Lill

Influence of Recommender Systems on Consumer Behavior

Series: Electronic Commerce & Digital Markets
Volume: 17
Editor: Prof. Dr. Martin Spann
ISSN: 2199-7608
ISBN: 978-3-7693-2848-6

Ludwig-Maximilians-Universität München
Munich School of Management
Institute of Electronic Commerce and Digital Markets
Geschwister-Scholl-Platz 1
80539 Munich
Germany
www.som.lmu.de/ecm

MARKUS LILL

Influence of Recommender Systems on Consumer Behavior

Foreword by Martin Spann

Imprint

Bibliographic information is published by Deutsche Nationalbibliothek.
The Deutsche Nationalbibliothek lists this publication in the Deutsche Nationalbibliografie;
Detailed bibliographic data are available on the internet at dnb.dnb.de

Author:
Dr. oec. publ. Markus Lill
E-Mail: markus.lill@gmx.de

Publisher: BoD · Books on Demand GmbH, In de Tarpen 42,
22848 Norderstedt, bod@bod.de
Print: Libri Plureos GmbH, Friedensallee 273, 22763 Hamburg
E-Mail: info@bod.de
Internet: www.bod.de

Dissertation 2025
LMU Munich/Ludwig-Maximilians-Universität München
Reference Number/Kennziffer: D 19
Foreword by Prof. Dr. Martin Spann

1st Edition 2025

Cover design & layout: Dr. Markus Lill
Cover image: © iStock.com/Rizwan12

Printed on FSC-certified paper.

ISSN 2199-7608
ISBN 978-3-7693-2848-6

Foreword

A key difference between online and brick-and-mortar retail is that online retailers can offer a much wider range of products because they are no longer limited to a physical store. The resulting need to help consumers find suitable products has led to the development and widespread use of recommendation systems.

Recommendation systems have a major impact on consumer search and decision-making. Much of the research to date in computer science, information systems, and related areas of business administration has focused on the development, predictive accuracy, and impact of recommendation systems on consumer decisions. Despite the extensive research interest in recommendation systems, two research gaps can be identified. First, the impact of recommendation systems on and their interaction with consumer behavioral biases has been relatively understudied. Second, research on recommendation systems is methodologically dominated by laboratory experiments or the use of secondary data, while field experiments have rarely been used.

Markus Lill's dissertation addresses both gaps by investigating the influence of recommendation systems on behavioral biases according to three core elements of recommendation systems: (i) the selection of products recommended to a consumer, (ii) the ordering of these products (e.g., ranking), and (iii) additional recommendation cues such as "best seller" or "Amazon's tip". Through several field experiments and the analysis of a large secondary data set, he shows how platforms use different choice architecture designs of recommendation systems, how they affect consumers' decisions, and how these decisions are affected by behavioral biases.

Markus Lill's dissertation is an important contribution to the theory and practice of recommendation systems. He successfully combines theories from behavioral economics with the design and implementation of field experiments in a digital platform environment. The results are highly relevant for vendors, consumers, and regulators who develop, deploy, and monitor recommendation systems.

Munich, February 2025   Martin Spann

Acknowledgements

Many individuals have accompanied and supported me throughout my academic journey, culminating in this dissertation. I am profoundly grateful for their support, guidance and encouragement.

First and foremost, I extend my deepest gratitude to my supervisor, Martin Spann. His expertise, insightful feedback, unwavering optimism, and patience have been invaluable to my research and this dissertation. I especially appreciate the trust he has given me in pursuing my ideas. I am also sincerely thankful to Thomas Hess for serving as co-referee of this dissertation and for his valuable comments.

I am particularly grateful to my co-authors, Nastasia Gallitz and Lucas Stich, whose contributions were indispensable to my research. Their time, thoughtful discussions, collaboration, and friendship have been immensely rewarding—along with the many moments of laughter we shared.

I would also like to express my appreciation to my colleagues at the Institute of Electronic Commerce and Digital Markets, many of whom have become dear friends. This journey would not have been as enjoyable without Camila Back, Sophie Berghüser, Walli Broch, Pauline Engel, Weilong (Mike) Gu, Alice Harter, Alexander Pfaff, Eva Pflanzer, David Prakash, Eva Schuhbeck, Emanuel Schuster, and Johanna Verenkotte. I have truly valued our time together and am grateful for their support and insightful feedback over the years.

Additionally, I am deeply grateful to our anonymous project partner for their valuable contributions and availability for insightful discussions. Their support greatly enhanced my understanding of the underlying information and business context, contributing significantly to my research.

Finally, I am profoundly grateful to my family and friends for their unwavering support and love. They believed in me, lifted me up when I needed encouragement, and reminded me to laugh regardless of the circumstances.

Munich, February 2025   Markus Lill

Influence of Recommender Systems on Consumer Behavior

Inaugural-Dissertation

zur Erlangung des Grades Doctor oeconomiae publicae (Dr. oec. publ.)

an der Ludwig-Maximilians-Universität München

vorgelegt von

Markus Lill

Jahr: 2024

Referent:	Prof. Dr. Martin Spann
Korreferent:	Prof. Dr. Thomas Hess
Promotionsabschlussberatung:	29.01.2025

Table of Contents

Introduction

1 Motivation and Objective

The advent and rapid development of modern technologies have transformed digital platforms, adding complex layers to consumer behavior and decision-making processes. Recommender systems (RSs) are one component of this digital transformation. RSs leverage consumer data and predictive algorithms to suggest content tailored to consumers' preferences (Resnick and Varian 1997, Adomavicius et al. 2018, Ricci et al. 2022). The application of RSs on digital platforms has become a fundamental part of retailers from various professions, including streaming services (Gomez-Uribe and Hunt 2015, Schedl et al. 2021), social networks (Aivazoglou et al. 2020), news platforms (Schmalenbach et al. 2022), or marketplaces (Linden et al. 2003), supporting consumers to navigate through the content catalog (Häubl and Trifts 2000).

Furthermore, digital platforms also incorporate product badges as supplementary RS tools to influence consumer behavior. Product badges, such as bestsellers, serve as visual indicators that highlight products, adding another layer of persuasion by reducing quality uncertainty and signaling popularity (Hui et al. 2016, Cheng et al. 2020). These badges complement recommendations to shape consumer decisions, often simplifying decision-making by offering easily recognizable visual cues that reduce search costs.

By utilizing RSs, retailers can often enhance their conversion rates and overall consumption (Li et al. 2022). Studies indicate that online retailers who successfully implement RSs can experience an increase in sales by influencing the consumer decision-making process (Schafer et al. 1999, Pathak et al. 2010, Lee and Hosanagar 2014). Furthermore, research suggests that RSs can decrease information overload and search complexity while enhancing the quality of consumer decisions (Maes 1995). However, RSs also shape consumer preferences, beliefs, and decision-making processes through the induction of behavioral biases

(DellaVigna 2009, Teppan and Zanker 2015). Behavioral biases, a crucial concept in consumer decision-making theory, are deviations from the standard economic model (Rabin 2002), often resulting in choices that divert from rational or optimal outcomes. Therefore, as RSs evolve and become increasingly integrated into online shopping platforms (Linden et al. 2003), understanding their impact on consumer behavior becomes a crucial area of investigation.

This dissertation aims to provide a comprehensive overview of how RSs induce behavioral biases and influence consumer behavior (see Article 1). Specifically, through field experiments, we investigate three different RS dimensions that shape consumer behavior: item selection (see Article 2 and Article 3), ranking (see Article 3) and recommendation design (see Article 4). We analyze how these RS dimensions can induce behavioral biases and affect consumer behavior. Despite the growing prevalence of RSs, insights from field experiments remain sparse. Therefore, this dissertation emphasizes a field-based approach to generate empirical evidence on how RS dimensions affect consumer behavior in real-world settings.

First, we conduct a systematic literature review of behavioral biases in RSs, establishing a foundation for understanding how RSs can influence consumer behavior. The first empirical paper builds on this foundation and explores the role of assimilation effects in RSs and their impact on overall RS acceptance. The study highlights how contextual similarity between recommended products and currently viewed items can shape consumer responses.

The following empirical work expands on assimilation effects, focusing on contrast effects among recommendations. Furthermore, the article examines the impact of position bias through recommendation ranking. Finally, the dissertation examines the influence of product badges on consumer search behavior and product choices on digital platforms. By investigating how these visual cues interact within RSs, this final study offers insights into how additional elements of platform design shape consumer behavior, rounding out the exploration of RSs' influence on consumer behavior.

2   Contribution of the Dissertation

This dissertation contributes to RS research in various ways. The following section provides an overview of each article's contribution.

Article 1 enriches the literature on RSs by providing a comprehensive overview of behavioral biases in RSs. By analyzing articles from various journals and conferences, this work categorizes behavioral biases induced by RSs along the three RS dimensions: item quantity and selection, item ranking, and explanation and reviews. Utilizing DellaVigna's (2009) framework, the article identifies how RSs can influence user preferences, beliefs and decision-making. It contributes to the field of RSs by providing a structured analysis of these biases and showing how they affect consumer behavior. Furthermore, the article sheds light on the different methodologies applied in RS research and reveals the limited empirical research, especially through field experiments.

Article 2 advances RS research by highlighting the significance of assimilation effects (Bless and Schwarz 2010) in shaping consumer behavior, particularly the role of contextual similarity between recommended and currently viewed products in retail e-commerce. Through empirical findings from a field experiment, the study adds to the understanding of how content-based RSs (Ricci et al. 2022) affect consumer behavior and increase click-through rates (CTRs), emphasizing the critical role of contextual alignment in RSs. This contribution challenges the dominant emphasis on diversity and serendipity in RS design (Kaminskas and Bridge 2016, Kotkov et al. 2016), suggesting that prioritizing similarity over diversity can be more effective in enhancing user engagement.

Article 3 deepens the understanding of position bias (Collins et al. 2018) and contrast effects (Bless and Schwarz 2010) in RSs, providing valuable insights into user behavior. Through a field experiment, the study challenges the conventional assumption that the top position is always the most effective (Collins et al. 2018, Ursu 2018), revealing that items in the second and third positions can generate higher CTRs. The research contributes to and validates the concept of local contrast (Häubl et al. 2010, Guo et al. 2023), which had previously only been confirmed in laboratory experiments. The study demonstrates that user decisions are influenced by comparisons with previously viewed items, thereby extending the application of contrast theory to RS contexts. Furthermore, the study contributes to RS design strategies by demonstrating how non-relevant but visually distinct recommendations can enhance the appeal of focal items (Rafai et al. 2022), offering practical insights into increasing the effectiveness of recommendations.

Article 4 enriches RS literature by exploring how product badges, such as Best Seller, act as cognitive shortcuts that influence consumer decision-making on digital platforms (Cheng et al. 2020). Existing studies primarily utilize experimental laboratory settings or secondary data analysis (Goodman et al. 2013, Hui et al. 2016, Cheng et al. 2020, Ghiassaleh et al. 2020). Article 4 provides robust external validity on how badges influence consumer search and choice behavior by conducting three field experiments. The research demonstrates how platform-endorsed badges guide consumer preferences in multi-badge environments. Popularity badges, such as Best Seller, gain prominence when other cues are absent. The article offers practical insights for platform managers on leveraging badges to optimize consumer engagement. It informs regulators on the implications of badge usage for fairness and transparency in digital marketplaces. Additionally, the article advances methodological approaches by introducing a software architecture for analyzing and conducting field experiments on digital platforms that future researchers can utilize.

Overall, this dissertation contributes to the RS literature by enhancing the external validity of findings through field experiments, which are relatively rare in RS research. By integrating established concepts like assimilation and contrast theory, which have been sparsely applied in RS contexts, the dissertation provides new insights into how contextual similarity and contrast shape consumer behavior. Moreover, it challenges traditional RS design priorities, such as the emphasis on diversity, by highlighting the effectiveness of similarity-based recommendations in specific retail environments. This work also offers valuable methodological advancements by developing tools for conducting field experiments, thus expanding the empirical foundations of RS research.

3 Dissertation Structure and Article Abstracts

This cumulative dissertation comprises four articles, integrated within a comprehensive introduction and conclusion, as depicted in Figure 1. The first article builds the foundation of the dissertation by providing a comprehensive literature overview of behavioral biases in RSs. Following this, three empirical articles provide insights from field experiments into the influence of RSs on consumer behavior.

Figure 1. Dissertation Structure

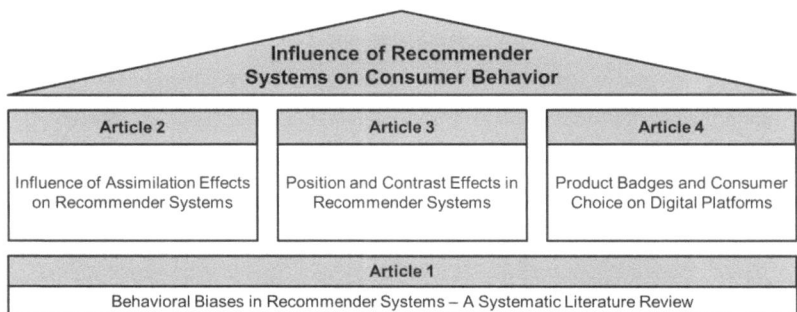

Each article's key findings, objectives, data, and methods are briefly outlined and presented in Table 1. Short summaries of the articles are provided at the end of this section.

Article 1 builds the theoretical foundation of the dissertation, aiming to provide an overview of identified behavioral biases within RSs. Through a systematic literature review of 43 articles from 31 journals and conference proceedings, the study summarizes insights and classifies them based on their impact on consumer preferences, beliefs, and decision-making. Along the three RS dimensions of item quantity and selection, item ranking, and explanations and reviews, this literature review analyzes how behavioral biases can be induced through RSs.

Article 2, the first of three empirical articles, examines the role of contextual similarity in RSs within retail e-commerce, focusing on how the alignment between recommended products and the context of the currently viewed item influences consumer behavior. Utilizing data from a midsize European retail company, a field experiment was conducted to investigate the role of assimilation effects between a focal item and its recommendations generated by an item-based collaborative filtering (IBCF) algorithm. The findings highlight that contextual similarities significantly enhance consumer click behavior, emphasizing the importance of these factors in optimizing RS performance.

Article 3 explores the impact of position and contrast effects on user decision-making within RSs, analyzing on how these factors can induce behavioral biases that influence consumer choices. Building upon the insights on assimilation effects from Article 2, the third article narrows the focus to contrast effects, specifically examining a single item from a list of recommendations. Through a field experiment, the study investigates how a specific recommendation's positioning and its contrasts with other IBCF recommendations affect user CTRs. The findings reveal that the strategic positioning of a highlighted focal item and its contrast with other recommendations significantly enhance its acceptance rate. Moreover, contrast that is induced by non-relevant recommendations further increases click probability. This study provides valuable insights for optimizing RS design, emphasizing the importance of strategic placement and diverse options to better align with user preferences and behaviors.

Finally, Article 4 adds insights into how digital platforms can influence consumer choice using product badges in RSs. The study complements the other two empirical articles by analyzing how badges serve as additional visual cues in RSs, guiding consumer behavior and decision-making. While previous research has focused on search rankings and recommendations, this study systematically examines the impact of product badges on consumer search behavior and product choices. By analyzing Amazon data and conducting three field experiments using a custom web browser extension to mask product badges, the study reveals significant differences in how various badges, such as "Amazon's Choice" and "Best Seller," affect consumer actions. The findings show that masking the Amazon's Choice badge decreases click and add-to-cart rates while masking the Best Seller badge increases these actions. This research deepens the understanding of the role that badges play in shaping consumer behavior on digital platforms, offering valuable implications for consumers, regulators, and sellers.

Despite their varying research objectives, data, and methodologies, the articles collectively focus on investigating the influence of RSs on consumer behavior. Moreover, they emphasize the significance of behavioral biases within RSs in shaping user decisions. The first two empirical articles explore two RS dimensions identified in Article 1, focusing on the selection of RS recommendations (Article 2 and Article 3) and the ranking of recommendations (Article 3). The last empirical article (Article 4) addresses another underexplored area in RS research by examining the impact of product badges on consumer behavior. Together, these studies provide a comprehensive understanding of how different dimensions within RS environments can induce behavioral biases and impact consumer behavior, offering valuable insights for enhancing the design and effectiveness of RS strategies across digital platforms.

Table 1. Overview of Research Objectives, Data and Methods

	Article 1	Article 2	Article 3	Article 4
Article	Behavioral Biases in Recommender Systems – A Systematic Literature Review	Influence of Assimilation Effects on Recommender Systems	Position and Contrast Effects in Recommender Systems	Product Badges and Consumer Choice on Digital Platforms
Research objective	Provide a systematic review of behavioral biases in recommender systems and derive avenues for future research	Analyze the impact of contextual similarity between a currently inspected item and recommended items on user click behavior	Investigate how position and contrast effects in recommender systems influence user click-through rates	Analyze how different product badges influence consumer search behavior and product choice on digital platforms
Data	Scientific publications in journals and conference proceedings collected from three databases (N = 43 articles published in 31 different outlets)	Experimental data from a field experiment on an apparel e-commerce website (N = 13,041 observations from 4,451 users)	Experimental data from a field experiment on an apparel e-commerce website (N = 26,973 observations from 8,751 users)	Web scraped data (N = 231,547) and experimental data from three field experiments on a digital marketplace platform (overall N = 14,094 observations from 833 users)
Method	Systematic literature review	Field experiment, logit regression with user random effects	Field experiment, logit regression with user random and fixed effects	Field experiment, logit regression with clustered standard errors

Article 1. Behavioral Biases in Recommender Systems – A Systematic Literature Review

Behavioral biases are pivotal in recommender systems (RSs) in shaping user interactions and outcomes. Understanding these biases is essential for improving the effectiveness and fairness of RSs. This systematic literature review comprehensively analyzes and categorizes biases within three fundamental dimensions: consumer preferences, beliefs, and decision-making. By analyzing various scholarly articles, this study identifies the prevalence and impact of behavioral biases in the context of RSs. It provides an up-to-date overview and categorization of current research articles analyzing behavioral biases in RSs. Among the dimensions of product quantity and selection, ranking and explanation and reviews of RSs, we explore how the identified biases influence user preferences, distort belief formation, and affect decision-making processes. Furthermore, we outline a research agenda, highlighting potential avenues for future research. This work provides an overview for researchers and practitioners to understand the nuanced interplay between human cognition and technological systems, contributing to understanding how RSs influence consumer behavior.

Article 2. Influence of Assimilation Effects on Recommender Systems

Recommender systems (RSs) are a common approach in retail e-commerce to support consumers in finding relevant products. Not surprisingly, user acceptance of personalized product recommendations tends to be higher, leading to higher click rates. Since contextual information also influences user search behavior, we analyze the importance of similarity between recommendations and the underlying context a currently inspected product provides. Using data from a midsize European retail company, we conduct a field experiment and investigate the role of similarities between focal product information and recommendations from a collaborative filtering algorithm. We find that contextual similarity, primarily visual similarity contributes much explanation to consumer click behavior, underlining the importance of contextual and content information in the RS's environment.

Article 3. Position and Contrast Effects in Recommender Systems

This study examines how position and contrast effects influence user decision-making within recommender systems (RSs). Since these effects can induce behavioral biases that impact consumer choices, understanding their influence on RS effectiveness is crucial. Utilizing a field experiment, we analyze how recommendation placement and contrasts affect user acceptance rates. Our findings reveal that both the position of a focal item and its distinction from contrasting products significantly enhance click-through rates (CTRs). Greater visual differences between the focal item and other recommendations, as well as contrast with previously encountered items, increase CTRs, indicating that users are more likely to engage with recommendations that stand out. Our results challenge the assumption that the highest position in a recommendation list is always the most beneficial, showing that lower positions can lead to higher CTRs. This study provides valuable insights for optimizing RS design, emphasizing the importance of strategic placement and diversity to improve decision outcomes.

Article 4. Product Badges and Consumer Choice on Digital Platforms

Digital platforms can strategically influence consumer behavior by shaping the search environment. While previous research has focused primarily on search rankings and recommendations, the effect of product badges has not been systematically studied. This paper investigates how platform-controlled product badges affect consumers' search behavior and product choices on a digital platform. We analyze Amazon data and conduct a series of field experiments using a custom web browser extension developed to experimentally mask badges during the shopping experience. We find considerable heterogeneity in the prevalence, placement, and co-occurrence of different badge types on Amazon. Our experimental studies show that in a multi-badge environment and controlling for product and search characteristics, masking all badges reduces the likelihood of click and add-to-cart for products that received the platform endorsement badge (Amazon's Choice), while increasing these likelihoods for products that received the popularity badge (Best Seller). In single-badge environments, the Best Seller badge significantly increases the likelihood of click and add-to-cart, while the Amazon's Choice badge has no significant effect when controlling for product and search characteristics. This research adds to our understanding of how platform-controlled badges affect consumer behavior and provides insights for consumers, regulators, and sellers in digital marketplaces.

References

Adomavicius G, Bockstedt JC, Curley SP, Zhang J (2018) Effects of online recommendations on consumers' willingness to pay. *Information Systems Research* 29(1):84-102.

Aivazoglou M, Roussos AO, Margaris D, Vassilakis C, Ioannidis S, Polakis J, Spiliotopoulos D (2020) A fine-grained social network recommender system. *Social Network Analysis and Mining* 10:1-18.

Bless H, Schwarz N (2010) Mental construal and the emergence of assimilation and contrast effects: The inclusion/exclusion model. *Advances in Experimental Social Psychology*, vol. 42 (Elsevier), 319-373.

Cheng HK, Fan W, Guo P, Huang H, Qiu L (2020) Can "gold medal" online sellers earn gold? The impact of reputation badges on sales. *Journal of Management Information Systems* 37(4):1099-1127.

Collins A, Tkaczyk D, Aizawa A, Beel J (2018) Position bias in recommender systems for digital libraries. *International Conference on Information* (Springer), 335-344.

DellaVigna S (2009) Psychology and economics: Evidence from the field. *Journal of Economic literature* 47(2):315-372.

Ghiassaleh A, Kocher B, Czellar S (2020) Best seller!? Unintended negative consequences of popularity signs on consumer choice behavior. *International Journal of Research in Marketing* 37(4):805-820.

Gomez-Uribe CA, Hunt N (2015) The netflix recommender system: Algorithms, business value, and innovation. *ACM Transactions on Management Information Systems (TMIS)* 6(4):1-19.

Goodman JK, Broniarczyk SM, Griffin JG, McAlister L (2013) Help or hinder? When recommendation signage expands consideration sets and heightens decision difficulty. *Journal of Consumer Psychology* 23(2):165-174.

Guo X, Wang L, Zhang M, Chen G (2023) First things first? Order effects in online product recommender systems. *ACM Transactions on Computer-Human Interaction* 30(1):1-35.

Häubl G, Trifts V (2000) Consumer decision making in online shopping environments: The effects of interactive decision aids. *Marketing Science* 19(1):4-21.

Häubl G, Dellaert BGC, Donkers B (2010) Tunnel Vision: Local Behavioral Influences on Consumer Decisions in Product Search. *Marketing Science* 29(3):438-455.

Hui X, Saeedi M, Shen Z, Sundaresan N (2016) Reputation and regulations: Evidence from eBay. *Management Science* 62(12):3604-3616.

Kaminskas M, Bridge D (2016) Diversity, serendipity, novelty, and coverage: a survey and empirical analysis of beyond-accuracy objectives in recommender systems. *ACM Transactions on Interactive Intelligent Systems (TiiS)* 7(1):1-42.

Kotkov D, Wang S, Veijalainen J (2016) A survey of serendipity in recommender systems. *Knowledge-Based Systems* 111:180-192.

Lee D, Hosanagar K (2014) Impact of recommender systems on sales volume and diversity. *Proceedings of the 35th International Conference on Information Systems.*

Li X, Grahl J, Hinz O (2022) How Do Recommender Systems Lead to Consumer Purchases? A Causal Mediation Analysis of a Field Experiment. *Information Systems Research* 33(2):620-637.

Linden G, Smith B, York J (2003) Amazon.com recommendations: Item-to-item collaborative filtering. *IEEE Internet computing* 7(1):76-80.

Maes P (1995) Agents that reduce work and information overload. *Readings in Human–Computer Interaction* (Elsevier), 811-821.

Pathak B, Garfinkel R, Gopal RD, Venkatesan R, Yin F (2010) Empirical analysis of the impact of recommender systems on sales. *Journal of Management Information Systems* 27(2):159-188.

Rabin M (2002) A perspective on psychology and economics. *European economic review* 46(4-5):657-685.

Rafai I, Babutsidze Z, Delahaye T, Hanaki N, Acuna-Agost R (2022) No evidence of attraction effect among recommended options: A large-scale field experiment on an online flight aggregator. *Decision Support Systems* 153(113672):1-11.

Resnick P, Varian HR (1997) Recommender systems. *Communications of the ACM* 40(3):56-58.

Ricci F, Rokach L, Shapira B (2022) *Recommender Systems Handbook* (Springer, Boston, MA, USA).

Schafer JB, Konstan J, Riedl J (1999) Recommender systems in e-commerce. *Proceedings of the 1st ACM Conference on Electronic Commerce*, 158-166.

Schedl M, Knees P, McFee B, Bogdanov D (2021) Music recommendation systems: Techniques, use cases, and challenges. *Recommender Systems Handbook*, vol. 3 (Springer), 927-971.

Schmalenbach K, Gengler E, Laumer S (2022) Promoting Diverse News Consumption Through User Control Mechanisms. *Proceedings of the 43rd International Conference on Information Systems.*

Teppan EC, Zanker M (2015) Decision Biases in Recommender Systems. *Journal of Internet Commerce* 14(2):255-275.

Ursu RM (2018) The power of rankings: Quantifying the effect of rankings on online consumer search and purchase decisions. *Marketing Science* 37(4):530-552.

Article 1:

Behavioral Biases in Recommender Systems - A Systematic Literature Review[1]

Markus Lill

Behavioral biases are pivotal in recommender systems (RSs) in shaping user interactions and outcomes. Understanding these biases is essential for improving the effectiveness and fairness of RSs. This systematic literature review comprehensively analyzes and categorizes biases within three fundamental dimensions: consumer preferences, beliefs, and decision-making. By analyzing various scholarly articles, this study identifies the prevalence and impact of behavioral biases in the context of RSs. It provides an up-to-date overview and categorization of current research articles analyzing behavioral biases in RSs. Among the dimensions of product quantity and selection, ranking and explanation and reviews of RSs, we explore how the identified biases influence user preferences, distort belief formation, and affect decision-making processes. Furthermore, we outline a research agenda, highlighting potential avenues for future research. This work provides an overview for researchers and practitioners to understand the nuanced interplay between human cognition and technological systems, contributing to understanding how RSs influence consumer behavior.

Keywords: Recommender systems, behavioral biases, consumer decision making, literature review

---

[1] This article is based on the following paper: Lill, M. (2024). Behavioral Biases in Recommender Systems – A Systematic Literature Review. *Working Paper, LMU Munich.*

1   Introduction

The proliferation of digital technologies has significantly altered the landscape of consumer interaction. Recommender systems (RSs) have emerged as a fundamental tool in this digital ecosystem, designed to enhance user experience by offering personalized product suggestions (Resnick and Varian 1997). These systems are driven by complex algorithms and vast datasets, enabling them to predict and adapt to individual preferences with increasing accuracy.

Since their inception, RSs have been adopted across various online platforms, including retail websites, streaming services, and social media (Aivazoglou et al. 2020, Schedl et al. 2021). Their primary function is to filter through vast content catalogs and present users with the most relevant options, facilitating decision-making processes and improving user satisfaction (Swaminathan 2003). However, as these systems have grown more sophisticated, they have also introduced challenges and complexities.

One critical area of concern is the influence of behavioral biases on the development and utilization of RSs. Behavioral biases are systematic deviations from rational judgment that influence how users perceive and interact with recommendations (Piramuthu et al. 2012, Teppan and Zanker 2015).

While the technological complexity of RSs continues to evolve, there is a growing recognition in both research and practice that behavioral biases can influence the effectiveness of these systems (Y. Wang et al. 2023). These biases can significantly impact the quality of recommendations, leading to outcomes that may not fully align with user preferences or needs. From a consumer perspective, biases can lead to suboptimal decisions. For instance, users might rely too heavily on the first few recommendations they see (Collins et al. 2018) or select items that confirm their existing beliefs (Schwind et al. 2012) rather than exploring a broader range of options that might better suit their needs.

Furthermore, since user decisions are fed back into the RS, these biases can, in turn, lead to biases in the calculation of new recommendations (Zheng et al. 2023). This feedback loop can augment the problem, potentially resulting in the underrepresentation of some items. This phenomenon is part of a broader concept known as RS fairness (Yalcin and Bilge 2022), where certain products or content may be systematically disadvantaged, affecting the RS's diversity. Understanding and addressing these issues is crucial for developing more effective and fair RSs.

This review aims to provide a comprehensive overview of identified biases within RSs from research domains in artificial intelligence, computer science, information systems, management, marketing and psychology. By systematically categorizing and analyzing these biases, we can offer valuable insights into their impact and prevalence. This detailed overview will help researchers and practitioners recognize and address the specific biases that affect RS designs. Furthermore, presenting an underlying concept of behavioral biases and clustering them into defined schemes can significantly enhance the understanding of future RS development. This structured approach not only aids in identifying the root causes of biases but also promotes the creation of more bias-aware RSs that cover multiple objectives rather than pure accuracy-optimized recommendations (Zaizi et al. 2023).

The remainder of this systematic literature review is structured as follows: Section 2 provides an overview of RS dimensions and outlines the concept of behavioral bias categorization according to DellaVigna (2009). Section 3 describes our methodological approach for identifying relevant RS literature. Section 4 summarizes the descriptive and main findings of the systematic literature review, structured according to the identified behavioral biases: nonstandard preferences, nonstandard beliefs, and nonstandard decision-making. In Section 5, we propose an agenda for future research. We conclude the review in Section 6.

2   Theoretical Foundation

To establish a foundation for categorizing behavioral biases and the influential dimensions of RSs, we present a comprehensive framework for bias categorization and an in-depth conceptualization of the various RS dimensions. We aim to systematically categorize the different types of behavioral biases and outline the specific characteristics of RSs that contribute to the emergence and reinforcement of these biases.

Figure 1. Influence of RS Dimensions on Behavioral Biases

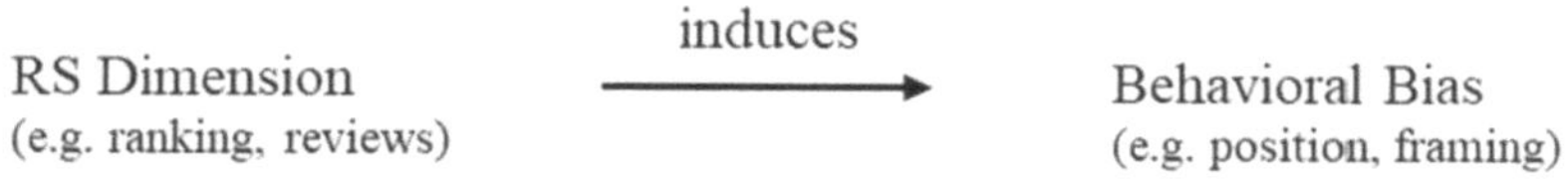

This systematic literature review focuses on the RS dimensions and the behavioral biases they induce (cf. Figure 1). Specifically, we analyze how various RS dimensions can potentially lead to specific behavioral biases.

2.1   Recommender System Dimensions

This section analyzes three dimensions that significantly impact the performance and user acceptance of RSs: the quantity and selection of recommended products, the ranking of these recommendations, and the explanations and consumer reviews provided to users. By examining these dimensions, we aim to provide a comprehensive overview of the elements that contribute to the influence of RSs on consumer behavior, offering insights into how these systems can potentially distort user behavior and lead to behavioral biases. See Figure 2 for an illustration of an RS implemented as a horizontal list on the bottom of a product detail page (PDP).

Figure 2. PDP With a List of Recommendations on the Bottom of the Page

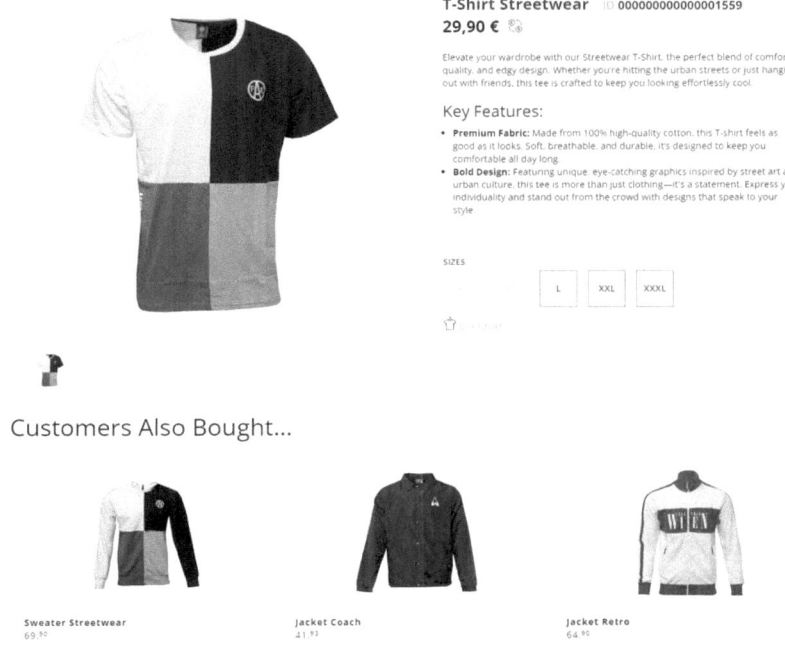

We chose these dimensions because they are fundamental to the user experience and directly influence the effectiveness of RSs. While other dimensions, such as users' data privacy concerns (Gulsoy et al. 2023), also play significant roles, they fall outside the scope of our current analysis. We focus on these selected dimensions because they represent the primary factors that are directly influenced by the RS design.

2.1.1   Item Quantity and Selection

RSs typically reduce the amount of products available to a more manageable subset, streamlining the consumer's decision-making process (Adomavicius and Tuzhilin 2005). This reduction involves filtering extensive product catalogs to a reduced selection of items. However, the RS objective is not to minimize the number of items to the smallest possible selection. It is also essential to retain a meaningful number of items for consumers to discover. The term "meaningful" (or sometimes "relevant") does not always refer to accuracy alone but can encompass other characteristics as well, like product catalog coverage or serendipity (Ge et al. 2010). Hence, no universal heuristic prescribes a fixed number of recommended items for all RS algorithms. Instead, the appropriate number of recommendations depends on the product catalog size, the specific algorithm, and the composition of product characteristics it considers.

However, RSs should filter the product catalog to a set of at least consumption-relevant items. Since the concept of relevancy is broad and includes various characteristics beyond accuracy (Kaminskas and Bridge 2016), other RS metrics have gained attention. For instance, novelty is crucial for discovering the latest items (L. Zhang 2013), particularly in news recommender systems. Diversity broadens the scope of user consumption, potentially opening new categories that can lead to higher profits (Smyth and McClave 2001). Serendipity enhances the entertainment and discovery aspects of RSs, helping to retain high engagement rates among consumers (Kotkov et al. 2016). Therefore, the characteristics of selecting items resulting from RSs vary and significantly influence how consumers interact with them.

2.1.2   Item Ranking

A fundamental task of RS algorithms is to calculate a metric for each product, reflecting the user's tendency toward item consumption. This can be achieved through various methods, such as estimating consumption probabilities, rating predictions, or assessing the similarity to previously consumed items (Aggarwal 2016).

While it might seem straightforward to rank items in descending order of their predicted consumption likelihood, many RSs employ reranking strategies to achieve a more nuanced approach (Pei et al. 2019). For instance, an RS algorithm might continuously predict very similar products. Therefore, identifying products with a lower rank (i.e., lower consumption tendency) that exhibit higher product diversity compared to other recommendations can enhance the overall diversity of the RS. This approach broadens the user's exploration and prevents the system from becoming monotonous (Vargas and Castells 2011).

More straightforward reranking strategies might also incorporate the release date of products to prioritize newer items (Vargas and Castells 2011), ensuring that the recommendations stay current and relevant. Various reranking algorithms are available, each designed to tackle different goals, such as enhancing the diversity of recommendations or balancing factors like novelty and relevance.

2.1.3   Explanation and Reviews

Most RSs provide explanations for their recommendations. These explanations might be statements like *"customers who bought [...] also bought [...]"* (cf. Linden et al. (2003)) or *"because you watched ..."* (cf. Gomez-Uribe and Hunt (2015)). The primary purpose of these explanations is to increase the acceptance of RSs by offering insights into data usage and creating consumer trust in the RS (W. Wang and Benbasat 2007). Providing clear and understandable explanations can help users trust the RS more and feel more comfortable following its suggestions. However, the specific design and wording of these explanations can significantly affect user behavior (Gai and Klesse 2019).

Another common feature in RSs is consumer reviews, which can be presented in various forms. One prevalent option is ratings, such as a five-star scale representing users' aggregated evaluations, providing a quantifiable measure of item quality and user preference (Li et al. 2022). Ratings serve a dual purpose: they are critical in calculating recommendations (Aggarwal 2016) and act as a persuasive factor for users considering a product (Jingjing Zhang 2011). User ratings are often displayed alongside recommendations.

We also include the impact of written consumer reviews on user behavior (Baum and Spann 2014). We only do this when the reviews are closely integrated and connected with the RSs, e.g., when provided on product detail pages. However, we do not analyze other product-specific characteristics like product descriptions or prices that would broaden the scope of this literature review beyond its intended focus. We aim to capture the most significant elements influencing how users interact with and perceive RSs by focusing on explanations and reviews.

2.2   Behavioral Biases Categorization

In behavioral economics and marketing, biases in consumer behavior are defined as deviations from the standard economic model (Rabin 2002). These biases significantly influence consumer decision-making processes, often resulting in choices that deviate from rational or optimal outcomes. Understanding these biases is essential for developing more effective marketing strategies and enhancing consumer satisfaction. Following the approach of Dowling et al. (2020) and utilizing the framework proposed by DellaVigna (2009), we categorize behavioral biases in RSs into three distinct types: nonstandard preferences, nonstandard beliefs, and nonstandard decision-making.

We utilize this classification for multiple reasons. First, the framework is rooted in well-established economic theory, providing a robust and widely accepted basis for categorizing behavioral biases. This theoretical foundation ensures that the classification is rigorous and credible. Second, this classification is not only applicable to economics but also intersects with marketing and consumer psychology. This interdisciplinary relevance allows for a more holistic understanding of biases, making it suitable for analyzing biases within RSs which are influenced by consumer interactions. Third, the structured nature of DellaVigna's (2009) classification facilitates a systematic and organized analysis. This approach enhances this review's clarity and ensures that all relevant biases are comprehensively covered and addressed.

Nonstandard Preferences

The first category of behavioral biases, known as nonstandard preferences, encompasses several deviations from the traditional economic model, like time-inconsistent, reference-dependent, and social preferences (DellaVigna 2009, Dowling et al. 2020). These biases potentially impact user interactions and decision-making processes.

In RSs, nonstandard preferences potentially shape user behavior and the overall effectiveness of the recommendations. In the context of RSs, *time-inconsistent preferences* may lead users to favor immediate, low-effort content over more valuable but time-consuming alternatives (Herings and Rohde 2006). *Reference-dependent preferences* mean users' satisfaction with recommendations might depend on reference points (Jindal 2015). Past experiences or expected outcomes potentially affect how consumers perceive and value new recommendations. Users might perceive recommendations that differ from their usual choices as "losses," leading them to favor familiar items even when new options could offer better utility. Finally, *social preferences* (Charness and Rabin 2002) can lead to biases where users are more likely to interact with recommendations that others in a community prefer.

Nonstandard Beliefs

The second category of deviations, nonstandard beliefs, arises when individuals encounter uncertainty in decision-making. Under such conditions, people form beliefs about potential outcomes or "states of the world" (Dowling et al. 2020). The standard economic model assumes that individuals accurately assess the distribution of these states and update their beliefs according to Bayes' rule as new information becomes available. However, empirical evidence indicates that consumers potentially form systematically inaccurate beliefs and do not behave as Bayesian information processors (Rabin 2002, DellaVigna 2009).

One belief-based bias is *overconfidence*, where users overestimate their ability to assess recommendations or predict outcomes (Moore and Healy 2008). Overconfidence may cause users to stick with their initial beliefs about their preferences, even when presented with new recommendations that contradict those beliefs. Another bias is *projection bias*, where users project their current state or preferences into the future (Conlin et al. 2007). In RSs, this might occur when users make choices based on the situational context in which recommendations are presented.

Nonstandard Decision-Making

This last category of deviations includes observations where individuals do not behave in a utility-maximizing manner due to the breakdown of several assumptions: namely, that people are fully informed, process information perfectly, and make decisions that are consistent across different contexts without being influenced by emotions (Bettman et al. 1998).

In the context of RSs, nonstandard decision-making plays a critical role in shaping user interactions and outcomes. One key aspect of nonstandard decision-making is the *framing effect*, where the way recommendations are presented influences user choices (Levin et al. 1998, Simonson 2008). Similarly, *context effects*, such as the *compromise* or *attraction effect* (Simonson 1989), can manipulate how users perceive recommended items. In the compromise effect, users may prefer middle-ground recommendations over extreme ones, while in the attraction effect, a less desirable recommendation makes a similar but superior item more appealing. Another factor that influences nonstandard decision-making is the *limited cognitive capacity* of users, which affects how consumers process recommendations (Simon 1955). Users may overlook relevant options when overwhelmed by the number of choices or focus too much on salient features, such as top-ranked items, leading to suboptimal decisions.

3   Research Methodology

Our research methodology is inspired by the framework proposed by Webster and Watson (2002). Our approach rests on five steps. Initially, we will define the scope of our analysis and the respective research disciplines. Second, we will identify the respective publication outlets. Third, we will define a set of electronic databases we utilize to screen literature with specific keywords. The fourth step involves a forward and backward search of the studies identified in the previous step. The last step covers analyzing and synthesizing the identified literature. The following section provides a detailed description of our methodology to ensure its transparency and replicability.

First, we identify the relevant research disciplines and publication outlets. RS research is an information systems (IS) topic. However, we are interested in the intersection between RSs and consumer behavior. Therefore, we do not limit our review to the IS field (Webster and Watson 2002) and extend our analysis to management, marketing and psychology disciplines. Furthermore, we will also include articles on artificial intelligence (AI) and computer science due to the advent of the latest insights from AI research and its close connection to RS development. Additionally, our goal is to assess the extent of empirical evidence regarding behavioral biases in the context of RSs. Hence, we focus exclusively on empirical and quantitative studies, excluding purely theoretical contributions and systematic literature reviews (e.g., Chen et al. (2023), Färber et al. (2023)).

Following the definition of research disciplines, we identify relevant journals based on the VHB-JOURQUAL 3 rating[2] (Schrader and Hennig-Thurau 2009) in the second step. We will only consider published articles in journals rated "C" or higher. For publications not listed in the VHB-JOURQUAL 3, we utilize

---

[2] https://vhbonline.org/service/vhb-jourqual/vhb-jourqual-3/gesamtliste

Clarivate's Journal Citation Report[3] (JCR) and consider journals with an impact factor of two or higher. We also include conference proceedings (Webster and Watson 2002), which align with one of the above metrics. Furthermore, we also include well-regarded conferences on computer science, especially in RSs (e.g., the ACM International Conference on Recommender Systems). Table A1 from the Appendix contains a complete list of journals and conferences.

Third, we define the databases we used to screen journals and conference proceedings identified in step two. We utilize three databases: EBSCO Business Source Complete, Clarivate's Web of Science and Elsevier's Science Direct. Since RS research has especially evolved in the past few years, we apply no temporal restriction and consider articles until the start of writing this essay in April 2024. To search for articles in the databases, we define a set of keywords. These keywords must be found in the article title, abstract or full text. We want to capture all articles that cover RS literature. Therefore, articles need to contain any of the terms "recommender system", "recommendation system" or "product recommendations". We also want to preselect articles potentially dealing with behavioral biases in RS literature. Hence, the keyword "bias" needs to occur with one of the previously mentioned RS keywords. We do not restrict "bias" further to ensure we cover as many behavioral biases within RS literature as possible.

Furthermore, we consider variations of those keywords that only slightly differ from the original ones. For example, we also consider plural versions like "recommender systems". We manually check all retrieved articles and create a list of unique articles from all three databases. From this list, we select only those articles that treat behavioral biases in RSs as a focal topic and exclude otherwise irrelevant articles. We remove pure algorithmic bias papers from our results since they do not incorporate the impact of biases on consumer behavior and only deal with technical advances and efficiency improvements in RSs. This also excludes

---

[3] https://jcr.clarivate.com/jcr/home

papers that purely focus on RS fairness which refers to algorithmic biases (process fairness) in the calculation of recommendations from user behavior or the underrepresentation of specific recommended items (outcome fairness) as a result of the RS (Y. Wang et al. 2023).

Fourth, we perform a forward and backward literature search after the manual check. As Webster and Watson (2002) mention, we examine the references of the identified literature from step three. Using Clarivate's Web of Science, we also search for citations for these articles. Additional literature found through forward and backward searches is included if it aligns with the journal requirements from step two and addresses the main topic.

Finally, similar to Dowling et al. (2020), we synthesize our findings on behavioral biases in RS literature according to the concepts defined by DellaVigna (2009) to provide a helpful overview of the clustering of the identified literature (Palmatier et al. 2018). To integrate the identified literature, we propose a classification scheme. Each discussed bias from our final article set is assigned to one of the three categories, according to DellaVigna (2009).

The first category contains nonstandard preferences, which include biases that deviate from the standard economic model of consistent and stable preferences. These biases reflect how external factors and psychological influences can alter consumer preferences in ways that traditional models do not account for. The second category covers nonstandard beliefs, which involve deviations in how individuals form and update their beliefs about the world. This includes biases where individuals' perceptions and interpretations of RS information are systematically distorted, affecting their belief formation. Finally, we cluster biases under nonstandard decision-making, encompassing deviations from rational decision-making models. These biases highlight how individuals' choices are influenced by cognitive limitations and contextual factors induced by the RS, leading to decisions that may not align with their best interests.

When multiple biases are considered in an article, we assign the specific paper to each relevant bias category separately, ensuring a comprehensive and nuanced classification of the literature. Hence, our structural scheme is not mutually exclusive, and some biases can also be assigned to multiple categories. For instance, biases due to framing also affect consumer beliefs. However, we use this classification framework to provide a structured analysis and clarify how these biases influence consumer behavior under RS usage. Table 1 provides an overview of the identified biases, categorized according to DellaVigna's (2009) concept.

Table 1. Examined Concepts within Properties of Behavioral Biases in RS According to Categorization by DellaVigna (2009)

Nonstandard Preferences (Section 4.2.1)	Nonstandard Beliefs (Section 4.2.2)	Nonstandard Decision-Making (Section 4.2.3)
• Social Influence and Conformity Bias	• Anchoring Effect	• Decoy Effect
• Popularity Bias	• Confirmation Bias	• Position Bias
• Filter Bubble and Echo Chamber	• Assimilation and Contrast Effect	• Choice Overload
		• Framing

It is essential to distinguish between algorithmic biases in RS and behavioral biases. For example, popularity bias can manifest as an algorithmic bias where the RS tends to recommend popular items rather than a behavioral bias where consumers inherently favor popular items. Therefore, we take particular care in differentiating between algorithmic and behavioral biases and acknowledge that some algorithmic biases can lead to behavioral biases.

4   Systematic Literature Review

4.1   Descriptive Results

The literature search and screening process was conducted in May 2024. This comprehensive search resulted in 1,567 unique articles. After focusing specifically on the intersection of RSs and behavioral biases and applying our inclusion criteria, we refined our dataset to 43 articles published between 2003 and 2024. These articles are published across 26 journals and five conference proceedings. Figure 3 provides an overview of the number of articles published per year.

Figure 3. Number of Articles per Year (N = 43)

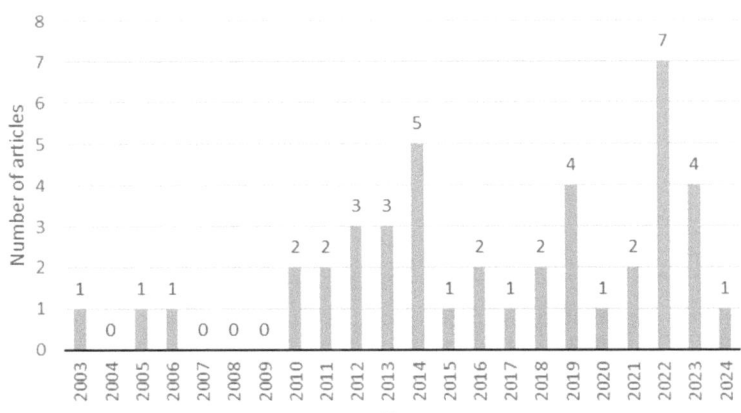

Our first identified paper is from 2003. Since RS research especially experienced growing interest in the past decade with the growing amount of content available on online platforms, research articles from the beginning of the 2000s or earlier are sparse. This is also reflected in our total article database from the initial screening process, with only 29 articles (~1.85%) published before 2003. Furthermore, most articles analyze algorithmic biases, such as RS fairness and metrics on identifying biases within RSs rather than their impact on consumer behavior.

We also identify two notable clusters of research articles, one around 2013 and another around 2022. The distribution of these identified articles follows the patterns observed in other comprehensive research studies on biases in RS research (cf. Chen et al. (2023) and Färber et al. (2023)), which also analyze biases more broadly, including algorithmic biases in addition to behavioral biases.

Possible explanations might be that around 2013, there may have been early recognition of behavioral biases in RSs, sparking academic curiosity and leading to foundational research. This period saw a growing number of studies presented at conferences and published in journals as the technology gained attention. Also, in recent years, the heightened emphasis on ethical AI might have prompted academia and industry to delve deeper into identifying and mitigating biases. This era likely marked an increase in interdisciplinary research, driven by the potential convergence of interests from computer science, psychology, and sociology. Combined with the release of ChatGPT in November 2022[4], this might be part of a possible explanation for the heightened interest in recent years[5].

We classified the identified articles according to the VHB-JOURQUAL 3 research discipline categorization. We referred to the JCR categories when journal or conference proceedings were not listed. Table 2 shows that most papers can be found within the research discipline of IS. This is unsurprising since RSs are integral to various IS applications, playing a crucial role in personalizing user experiences and enhancing decision-making processes across numerous digital platforms.

---

[4] https://openai.com/index/chatgpt/
[5] Note that we only cover articles from the first four months of 2024. Additional relevant articles on consumer biases in RS may be published later that year, increasing the total number of identified articles from 2024.

Table 2. Articles by Research Field / Discipline and Categorization According to DellaVigna (2009)

Research Field / Discipline	# Articles	Nonstandard Preferences	Nonstandard Beliefs	Nonstandard Decision-Making
Artificial Intelligence	3	2	0	2
Computer Science	3	1	1	1
Information Systems	18	7	7	5
Management	3	0	0	3
Marketing	7	1	2	6
Multidisciplinary	3	1	1	1
Psychology	2	1	1	0
Recommender Systems	4	1	1	2
Total	**43**	**14**	**13**	**20**

Notes. Rows do not add up to the number of articles in the first column since articles may cover multiple biases from different categories.

Interestingly, research from the marketing discipline demonstrates a focus on nonstandard decision-making, emphasizing how behavioral biases influence consumer choices and interactions with RSs. This finding aligns with the marketing interest in understanding and leveraging consumer decision-making. A detailed overview of the analyzed biases, RS dimension, and methodology per article can be found in the Appendix in Table A2.

4.2   Behavioral Biases in Recommender Systems

In the subsequent sections, we conduct an in-depth analysis of the identified literature for each behavioral bias categorized according to DellaVigna (2009).

4.2.1   Nonstandard Preferences

4.2.1.1   Social Influence and Conformity Bias

Social influence in RSs refers to the phenomenon where consumers align their preferences with those of friends, peers, or a broader community, even if these contradict their judgment (T. Wang and Wang 2014, Zhao et al. 2022). This behavior is driven by the desire for conformity, where individuals adjust their actions to match group norms. Hence, conformity bias is also closely related to social influence, as it arises when individuals adopt the preferences of others rather than relying on their preferences (Su et al. 2023).

Social influence can alter user preferences and their evaluations of products after experiencing them. Liu et al. (2016) highlight that users' initial judgments can be reshaped through social influence, leading to preference formation and post-consumption evaluation changes. This effect is also known as *herd mentality*, where consumers imitate and adjust their ratings to align with those of their peers, perceiving the group opinion as a safer and more reliable choice than their personal preferences (T. Wang and Wang 2014, Su et al. 2023).

Furthermore, the influence of prior ratings also impacts users' perceptions of the quality of recommendations (T. Wang and Wang 2014). Experimental research by Baum and Spann (2014) demonstrates that positive consumer reviews can increase the acceptance rate and purchase probability of recommended items when presented alongside recommendations. Conversely, negative reviews may reduce the acceptance of otherwise relevant recommendations, even if informative. The alignment between reviews and recommendations is crucial for inducing social influence, as mismatched feedback can weaken its effect.

Moreover, the effect of social influence is amplified by the tendency of consumers to provide reviews on items from trusted domains (Sánchez-Moreno et al. 2020). This feedback loop reinforces the exposure to items preferred by peers, as user reviews are fed back into the RS, promoting items from these trusted sources, which can lead to popularity bias (see 4.2.1.2) due to the overrepresentation of specific items (Zhao et al. 2022).

Social influence is also reflected in framing effects (see 4.2.3.4), where recommendations labeled as "user-based" tend to generate higher acceptance and click-through rates (Gai and Klesse 2019). When recommendations are perceived as being endorsed by other users, individuals are more likely to accept them, as their personal preferences are perceived to match the tastes of the broader community. This effect is even more substantial when group affiliation is emphasized, for example, through statements like "People who like this also like..." which further reinforces the perception of shared preferences within the user community.

4.2.1.2   Popularity Bias

Popularity bias occurs when users prefer popular items, accepting them regardless of their relevance (Wei et al. 2022). While popularity bias is mainly considered from an algorithmic perspective, there is also growing recognition in research that it manifests as a behavioral bias. Unlike social influence (see 4.2.1.1), where the bias stems from the popularity of an item among peers, popularity bias is induced by the inherent popularity of the item itself, often referred to as "item popularity" (Su et al. 2023).

Wei et al. (2022) argue that there is a behavioral tendency for consumers to prefer popular items over lesser-known ones. This inherent preference for popular items suggests that users are drawn to the security and familiarity of widely accepted options. Users who are easily satisfied tend to gravitate toward well-rated, popular items, avoiding the perceived risks of engaging with unfamiliar content (Yalcin and Bilge 2022). Since popular items are widely accepted within the community, users feel more confident choosing them, reducing the perceived risk of evaluating unknown items.

Interestingly, despite being framed as negative, popularity bias can also signal item quality. Zhao et al. (2022) suggest that users often perceive heavily consumed items as being of higher quality, implying that popularity can act as a heuristic for assessing product value. However, this behavioral bias is often reinforced by the algorithmic design of RSs. Melchiorre et al. (2023) highlight that RSs frequently recommend popular items. Even when users seek to explore new options, they often revert to popular items, resulting in overconsumption patterns that can perpetuate the exposure to similar popular items. This cyclical behavior can ultimately lead to filter bubbles (see 4.2.1.3), where users are repeatedly exposed to the same popular content, limiting their exposure to alternatives (Zhou et al. 2023).

4.2.1.3   Filter Bubble and Echo Chambers

Filter bubbles, sometimes referred to as echo chambers, describe the phenomenon where user preferences are increasingly reinforced over time as they are exposed to similar content (Zhou et al. 2023). This leads to narrowing consumer preferences and reducing exposure to diverse recommendations. RSs often intensify filter bubbles by consistently promoting content that aligns with users' past behaviors, further reinforcing their preferences.

Dandekar et al. (2013) emphasize that RSs can contribute to polarization by grouping users with similar opinions. This clustering effect reinforces users' existing preferences and reduces their exposure to alternative perspectives, deepening the filter bubble and limiting the diversity of consumed content.

However, research by Lee and Hosanagar (2014; 2019) reveals a more nuanced effect of RSs on content diversity. While RSs can increase individual consumption diversity by exposing users to higher content variety, this often comes at the expense of aggregate consumption diversity. While individual users may consume a broader range of items, RS algorithms push users towards a smaller set of popular items, resulting in a concentration of consumed content. This trend is closely connected to popularity bias (see 4.2.1.1), as the focus on popular items reduces overall diversity and contributes to forming filter bubbles at the aggregate level.

4.2.2   Nonstandard Beliefs

4.2.2.1   Anchoring Bias

Anchoring bias occurs when consumers rely heavily on the first information they encounter when evaluating alternatives (Adomavicius et al. 2013), which affects their belief formation. In the context of RSs, this bias is particularly relevant as users often base their decisions on the initial ratings or recommendations presented to them.

Anchoring bias in RSs can significantly influence consumer beliefs, mainly when ratings displayed to users serve as reference points that shape their subsequent choices (Köcher et al. 2019). Adomavicius et al. (2013) demonstrate that RS ratings often act as anchors for consumer beliefs. However, the strength of this effect is linked to the perceived RS reliability. Higher RS reliability leads to higher anchoring effects, as users are more likely to perceive the provided rankings as the "correct" ratings for specific recommendations. Conversely, the anchoring bias diminishes when recommendations are labeled as "tentative" or when the RS is described as being in a test phase (Jingjing Zhang 2011).

Furthermore, Adomavicius et al. (2013) indicate that anchoring occurs after a decision is made and can influence consumer beliefs during the consumption process. This suggests that anchoring bias can have a lasting effect on user beliefs, shaping their perceptions even after they have begun interacting with the recommended item.

In another study, Adomavicius et al. (2019) also find that the type of RS rating display can impact the extent of anchoring bias. Numerical rating displays, such as star ratings, are more prone to inducing anchoring effects than graphical representations like thumbs up/down or bar displays. However, neither type of display can eliminate anchoring bias. Furthermore, the bias is amplified when the rating display and the consumer response tool share the same format.

Finally, anchoring bias can also be linked to assimilation effects (see 4.2.2.3), where one item's ratings influence subsequent items' evaluation. Z. Yang et al. (2013) find that users tend to rate items that follow low-rated items more negatively, while items following higher-rated ones tend to receive higher ratings.

4.2.2.2   Confirmation Bias

Confirmation bias occurs when users prefer information that aligns with their beliefs, leading them to engage more frequently with content that reinforces those beliefs (Tang and Wu 2022). This effect can cause a loop where users' pre-existing beliefs are reinforced over time through RS interactions (see 4.2.1.3). Schwind et al. (2012) frame this bias in terms of "preference", though they also mention that "knowledge" influences user decisions. Therefore, we refer to this phenomenon as a bias in "belief" since it extends beyond preferences.

Confirmation bias is pronounced in environments where users hold prior opinions, which leads them to disregard or downplay recommendations that challenge their beliefs. Schwind and Buder (2012) find that when users are presented with options that conflict with their beliefs, they are more likely to interact with belief-consistent content. However, their research suggests that deliberately displaying belief-inconsistent recommendations can help mitigate confirmation bias. In some cases, this can result in an inversion of the confirmation bias effect on consumers: more open-minded users prefer belief-inconsistent recommendations when they are flexible about their beliefs.

Ho et al. (2017) explore confirmation bias within the context of online rating behaviors. Their study reveals that users who experience disconfirmation are more likely to post reviews that reflect their initial beliefs rather than their experience. This behavior further enhances confirmation bias, as the content of these reviews is shaped more by users' pre-existing beliefs than by their interactions with the product or service.

Furthermore, Eryarsoy and Piramuthu (2014) find that the order in which reviews are read can significantly influence users' perceptions and subsequent reviews. This sequence can lead users to reinforce the prevailing sentiment in a set of reviews, further enhancing confirmation bias in RSs as users unintentionally contribute to reinforcing initial impressions.

Additionally, Tang and Wu (2022) study confirmation bias in the context of congenial and uncongenial reviews. They find that positive reviews that align with users' prior attitudes are perceived as more credible and less subjective, reinforcing confirmation bias, especially among highly involved users. Their findings indicate that confirmation bias leads to stronger positive judgments of favored titles, while negative reviews have a lesser impact on users who already hold positive prior attitudes.

4.2.2.3   Assimilation and Contrast Effect

Assimilation and contrast effects are considered behavioral biases because they demonstrate how prior information and the context in which recommendations are presented can significantly skew user perceptions and beliefs about recommendations (Bless and Schwarz 2010). These biases arise from how users relate new information to what they have previously encountered.

While often categorized alongside anchoring bias (see 4.2.2.1), assimilation effects occur when users pay more attention to product alternatives similar to the recommendations they have seen, making them more likely to accept items with similar attributes (Köcher et al. 2019). This tendency to favor recommendations resembling previously explored products influences consumer acceptance of subsequent recommendations (Lill and Spann 2022). Visual similarity and product category overlap are two important drivers. Users prefer products that look similar to previously inspected products or share the same product categories.

On the other hand, contrast effects can arise when there are noticeable differences between previously viewed recommendations and a currently inspected product. This can result in users overestimating the attractiveness of the currently investigated product due to the contrast with previous recommendations (Häubl et al. 2010).

Moreover, highly relevant recommendations can benefit from the influence of previously inspected products, especially when the items are difficult to evaluate. Guo et al. (2023) find that if the most relevant recommendation is not the first product a user encounters, its attractiveness can increase due to the comparison with earlier explored items.

4.2.3   Nonstandard Decision-Making

4.2.3.1   Decoy Effect

Decoy effects can occur when an additional item is introduced to a list of recommendations to increase the attractiveness of certain products. Two of the most well-researched decoy effects in consumer decision-making are asymmetric dominance (Huber et al. 1982) and the compromise effect (Simonson 1989). Even though RSs are designed to provide relevant products to consumers, introducing decoy items can sometimes improve the decision-making process by guiding users toward a target option (Teppan et al. 2011). However, this comes at the cost of deliberately introducing an item that potentially causes behavioral biases in RSs.

Teppan and Zanker (2015) demonstrate that including decoy items in RSs can increase the acceptance of a specific target item. Their findings indicate that the effectiveness of decoy effects is context-dependent, being more robust in scenarios where consumers are risk-seeking. Despite these findings, studies have shown that decoy effects are not consistently observed in RSs. A field study by Rafai et al. (2022) could not verify the presence of attraction effects induced by decoy items. Their results could not confirm increased CTRs for product alternatives when displaying a decoy item.

Furthermore, research by Mousavi et al. (2021) indicates that RS's effectiveness can decrease when decoy items are introduced. This reduction in acceptance may be due to a perceived decrease in the RS's reliability, as consumers often view decoy items as irrelevant to their needs. This aligns with their findings that introducing decoy items does not significantly affect the overall acceptance of non-personalized RSs, where users have lower expectations for personalized relevance.

4.2.3.2   Position Bias

Position bias is a phenomenon where user decisions are influenced more by the placement of items in a recommendation list than by the items' relevance (Bian et al. 2012, Collins et al. 2018). This bias often arises because users rely on cognitive shortcuts and perceptual tendencies, leading them to favor items in certain positions. While highly ranked items can help reduce consumer search costs for relevant products (Ursu 2018), they can also bias consumer decision-making by causing users to prioritize items based on their placement rather than their relevance or personal fit.

Research consistently shows that items in higher positions are more likely to be selected, a trend attributed to the *primacy effect* (Murphy et al. 2006), where the first items seen are the most memorable and influential. Collins et al. (2018) find that items positioned at the top of recommendation lists receive more clicks, regardless of their relevance. Similarly, Lerman and Hogg (2014) demonstrate that items at the top of a list are clicked five times more often than those in lower positions, primarily due to the increased ease of access. Furthermore, Ursu (2018) notes that the higher visibility of top-ranked items directly contributes to higher CTRs.

The primacy effect is particularly noticeable when users need to put in more effort to make their decisions (Teppan and Zanker 2015). Bian et al. (2012) introduced the term "position decay factor" to describe the decline in click probability as items are lower ranked, regardless of their relevance. Users often follow a linear inspection pattern and may stop exploring early, assuming low-ranked items are less likely to be useful (Melchiorre et al. 2023).

Items at the bottom of a list can sometimes benefit from the *recency effect*, where the last items viewed leave a stronger impression. However, this effect is generally weaker than the primacy effect (Murphy et al. 2006). Teppan and Zanker (2015) find that although recency effects exist, primacy effects dominate online shopping scenarios.

Items positioned neither at the top nor the bottom of the list can also benefit from the effects of comparative evaluation, often linked to contrast effects. Häubl et al. (2010) find that placing items in the middle of a list could impact user perceptions through comparisons with previously viewed products. This comparative evaluation can shape decision-making, as users are more likely to assess middle-ranked items to what they have already seen. Guo et al. (2023) further suggest that placing the most relevant recommendation in the second position can facilitate better product comparisons, resulting in improved decision outcomes and higher acceptance rates.

4.2.3.3   Choice Overload

One of the most significant contributions of RSs to digital platforms is their ability to help users navigate through product catalogs by filtering products of interest (Adomavicius and Tuzhilin 2005). However, consumers often prefer to choose from large assortments, even if they find it challenging to evaluate all the options available (Chernev 2003). This creates a paradox: users are drawn to larger assortments but may struggle with decision-making when faced with too many options.

As the number of recommendations increases, so does the difficulty of making a decision. Bollen et al. (2010) find that while choice difficulty increases when users are presented with 20 recommendations compared to five, consumer satisfaction remains unchanged across different set sizes. Interestingly, decision difficulty decreased when less relevant recommendations were introduced, but so did consumer satisfaction, indicating that relevance is a critical factor in user contentment (see 4.2.3.1, the influence of irrelevant items).

This finding aligns with the work of Willemsen et al. (2016), who show that larger and more diverse recommendation lists can increase user satisfaction. Even though users have to evaluate a broader range of product attributes, the diversity of the options presented leads to higher satisfaction levels.

However, larger recommendation lists can also result in poorer choices. Diehl (2005) pointed out that RSs first present the most relevant recommendations. Items in lower ranks are more likely to be less relevant and of lower quality. However, users who are motivated to make accurate and high-quality decisions may explore lower-ranked items. Hence, this exploration often leads to suboptimal choices as these recommendations are less fitting. This highlights a challenge in RS design: balancing the desire for variety and large assortments with the need to ensure the quality and relevance of recommendations to prevent choice overload.

4.2.3.4   Framing

Framing effects refer to the phenomenon where consumers make different decisions based on how options are presented. Grounded in Kahneman and Tversky's (1979) Prospect Theory, framing can influence whether users behave in a risk-seeking manner (when options are framed as losses) or risk-averse manner (when options are framed as gains). In RSs, recommendations are often framed as gains, as this approach motivates users to buy or consume a product (Teppan and Zanker 2015).

This strategic use of framing can increase the acceptance rate of recommendations and boost the selection probability for specific products. Framings in RSs can take various forms, such as item-based framing, where product characteristics are highlighted (e.g., "New product entries..."), or user-based framing, which emphasizes similarities between consumers (e.g., "Consumers who bought... also bought...") (Gai and Klesse 2019).

Research shows that user-based framing is generally more effective, resulting in higher CTRs than item-based framing. User-based framing helps reduce the uncertainty about liking a recommended item by indicating user taste matching. However, the impact of this effect diminishes for users with more consumption experience or when the framing comes from demographically different groups (Gai and Klesse 2019).

Deng and Chau (2021) find that user- and item-based framings lead to higher CTRs than neutral framings. While they do not observe a significant difference in CTRs between user-based and item-based framings, they note that user-based framings enhance the perceived usefulness of the RS by signaling product similarity and shared preferences with other customers (see 4.2.1.1).

Further research by Junhui Zhang et al. (2022) confirms the heightened effectiveness of user-based framing, especially when only a few recommendations or substitutable products are presented. This suggests that user-based framing is most impactful in scenarios with limited choices, where users rely on the perceived similarity of preferences.

Additionally, recent findings by Y. Yang et al. (2024) highlight the potential downsides of AI-framed recommendations. They find that AI framing can negatively influence purchase intentions compared to human framing. However, when AI is "humanized" by being perceived as having higher warmth and competence, it can lead to an increased willingness to pay, demonstrating that the way AI recommendations are framed plays a crucial role in consumer decision-making.

5   Research Agenda

Based on the results of the systematic literature, we identify several avenues for future research. We classify them according to our structure of behavioral bias classification, RS dimensions, and methodology.

Table 3. Overview of Potential Research Questions and Recommendations

Avenues for Future Research	Potential Research Questions and Recommendations
Nonstandard Beliefs in RS	• How do contextual effects such as assimilation and contrast effects influence consumers' beliefs and perceptions of RSs? • How do recommendations for specific items shape consumer beliefs beyond overall acceptance, and how do these influences interact with other recommendations presented in a RS list?
Additional RS Dimensions	• How do product badges, such as Best Seller, influence consumer decision-making, and how do they impact the overall effectiveness of recommendations? • How does the interaction between product badges and other RS dimensions reflect in consumer behavior, and how can these interactions be explained?
Methodology and Data Sources	• Conduct field experiments and combine insights from multiple data sources (e.g., observational and experimental data) to overcome methodological limitations. • Generate field insights on consumer behavior on large digital platforms through modern software tools.

Nonstandard Beliefs in RS

Although literature explores contextual effects in RSs, understanding how the RS environment shapes consumer behavior remains limited. Specifically, research on behavioral biases in consumer nonstandard beliefs, such as assimilation and contrast effects, within the RS context is sparse (Häubl et al. 2010, Guo et al. 2023).

Further research should focus on how specific items within a list of recommendations can create a contextual environment that influences user beliefs and preferences. For example, items positioned closely within a recommendation list may benefit from perceived similarities, enhancing their acceptance. Conversely, differences among recommended items could trigger contrast effects, leading users to favor one option. In line with current research, the relationship between recommended items, whether through similarities or differences in product attributes, can significantly affect consumer beliefs and decision-making processes (Köcher et al. 2019, Guo et al. 2023). Future research could deepen our understanding of how specific items are evaluated within the broader recommendation environment by exploring how RSs can leverage these competing effects.

Additional RS Dimensions

As outlined in the systematic literature review, RSs have the potential to induce behavioral biases across multiple dimensions, including item selection and quantity, ranking, and explanations and reviews. Additionally, one increasingly common visual cue in RSs is using product badges, such as "Best Seller" which can influence consumer perceptions and decision-making. However, despite the extensive literature on badges and other visual cues (Bairathi et al. 2022, Dewan et al. 2023), there is limited research on how these elements interact with RSs.

Two competing mechanisms are at work: RSs aim to present relevant options, while product badges highlight specific items within those recommendations. These two elements, designed to enhance user acceptance and guide decision-making, may compete. The interaction between RSs and badges raises questions about how they influence consumer behavior. Specifically, it is important to explore whether badges reinforce or undermine the recommendations provided by the RS and how users navigate the interplay between these two systems. Further research is needed to explore this dynamic and to optimize the combination of RSs and visual cues like product badges to improve overall user experience and decision outcomes.

Methodology and Data Sources

The descriptive statistics of the identified literature reveal a reliance on laboratory experiments and secondary data analysis in RS research. Of the 43 articles examined, only nine utilized field experiments. Most studies rely on laboratory settings (21 articles) or secondary data analysis (11 articles). Laboratory experiments offer high internal validity, enabling researchers to control variables, examine causal effects, and explore the behavioral mechanisms underlying consumer behavior. However, they are limited in terms of external validity, as findings may not be generalized to real-world settings.

Similarly, while secondary data analysis provides valuable insights into user behavior across large datasets, it often lacks the experimental control necessary to identify causal relationships. These analyses are limited by the nature and quality of the available data, which may not capture all relevant behavioral dynamics or the context in which decisions are made.

We emphasize incorporating field experiments in RS research to address these limitations. Field experiments can provide valuable real-world insights by testing hypotheses in common settings, enhancing the external validity of findings. Combining field experiments with data from digital platforms, particularly through modern software tools (e.g., compare Farronato et al. (2023)), offers a promising approach. This integration allows researchers to generate insights that maintain the rigor of controlled experimentation and capture the complexity of real-world consumer behavior.

6   Conclusion

This systematic literature review highlights the multifaceted nature of behavioral biases within RSs, revealing how various RS dimensions can induce biases and influence consumer behavior. Each identified bias significantly shapes user formations of preferences, beliefs, and decision-making when using RSs. The insights drawn from the literature demonstrate that while RSs are important tools for enhancing user experience and decision-making, they also carry the potential to induce and reinforce biases that may influence consumer behavior.

We contribute to RS research in multiple ways. We provide a systematic literature review in which we identified and analyzed 43 articles from 31 journals and conference proceedings between 2003 and 2024. We identify ten of the most prevalent biases within RS research. We categorize each bias within the classification framework provided by DellaVigna (2009) into nonstandard preferences, nonstandard beliefs, or nonstandard decision-making and provide three different RS dimensions that induce these biases. Furthermore, we summarize and analyze the findings and provide detailed, empirically supported insights.

These findings have significant theoretical implications. Much of the research on optimizing RS accuracy overlooks the potentially harmful biases these systems can induce. However, there is a growing recognition within RS research to develop debiasing strategies that reduce the induction of behavioral biases through RS design (Boratto et al. 2021, Chen et al. 2023). Such strategies are essential to mitigate the unintended consequences of biased consumer behavior, ensuring RSs deliver relevant content and promote fairness, diversity, and user satisfaction. By addressing these biases, researchers can enhance the overall trustworthiness of RSs and prevent them from reinforcing existing inequalities or limiting users' exposure to diverse content.

Furthermore, while laboratory experiments and secondary data analyses have provided valuable insights, there is a clear need for more field experiments to enhance the external validity of these findings. Our systematic review reveals that much of the current knowledge is drawn from controlled settings, which may not fully capture real-world consumer behavior. Conducting field experiments will be essential to developing a more nuanced understanding of how RS-induced biases play out in practice.

From a managerial perspective, understanding these biases offers opportunities to direct consumer decision-making in the desired directions. For instance, leveraging position bias can be a simple yet effective tool for guiding consumers toward certain items without requiring substantial changes to existing RS implementations (Guo et al. 2023). However, this potential must be balanced against ethical considerations, as biases can also be used to manipulate consumer choices in ways that may not align with their interests.

Regulators should also be mindful of the implications of behavioral biases, especially given the prevalence of RSs on digital platforms. Most regulatory attention has focused on the selection and ranking mechanisms that drive RS outputs. However, other elements, such as how recommendations are explained to users, can also influence consumer choices and steer them toward platform-preferred items. As RSs continue to play a central role in shaping digital interactions, a deeper understanding of these biases will be critical for both managers and policymakers seeking to ensure that RSs are used responsibly and effectively.

Appendix

Table A1. Journal / Conference Name, Disciplines, Rating and Number of
Publications, N = 43

Journal Name / Conference Proceeding	Research Field / Discipline	Impact Factor[a] (VHB Rating[b])	Number of Articles
ACM Transactions on Computer-Human Interaction	Information Systems	4.8 (B)	1
Behavioral Sciences	Psychology	2.5	1
Big Data	Computer Science	2.6	1
Computers & Education	Computer Science	8.9	1
Computers in Human Behavior	Psychology	9.0	1
Decision Support Systems (DSS)	Marketing	6.7 (B)	1
EPL	Multidisciplinary	2.0	1
IEEE Transactions on Knowledge and Data Engineering	Artificial Intelligence	8.9	2
Information	Information Systems	2.4	1
Information & Management	Information Systems	8.2 (B)	1
Information Processing & Management	Information Systems	7.4	1
Information Systems Research	Information Systems	5.0 (A+)	4
International Journal of Electronic Commerce	Information Systems	4.2 (B)	1

Journal Name / Conference Proceeding	Research Field / Discipline	Impact Factor[a) (VHB Rating[b)])	Number of Articles
International Journal of Multimedia Information Retrieval	Artificial Intelligence	3.6	1
Journal of Business Research	Management	10.5 (B)	2
Journal of Computer-Mediated Communication	Information Systems	5.4 (C)	1
Journal of Consumer Research	Marketing	5.7 (A+)	1
Journal of Internet Commerce	Management	4.1	1
Journal of Marketing	Marketing	11.5 (A+)	1
Journal of Marketing Research	Marketing	5.1 (A+)	1
Journal of Retailing	Marketing	8.0 (A)	1
Management Information Systems Quarterly (MISQ)	Information Systems	7.0 (A+)	1
Marketing Science	Marketing	4.0 (A+)	2
Online Information Review	Information Systems	3.1	1
PLoS One	Multidisciplinary	2.9	1
Proceedings of the ACM Conference on Recommender Systems (RecSys)	Recommender Systems	na[c)	4

Journal Name / Conference Proceeding	Research Field / Discipline	Impact Factor[a] (VHB Rating[b])	Number of Articles
Proceedings of the International Conference on Information Systems (ICIS)	Information Systems	(A)	4
Proceedings of the National Academy of Sciences of the United States of America	Multidisciplinary	9.4	1
Proceedings of the Pacific Asia Conference on Information (PACIS)	Information Systems	(C)	1
Security and Communication Networks	Information Systems	2.0	1
User Modeling and User-Adapted Interaction	Computer Science	3.0	1
Total			**43**

Notes. [a]Impact Factor (2023) retrieved from https://jcr-clarivate-com.emedien.ub.uni-muenchen.de/jcr/home. [b]VHB Rating provided when available. [c]Not applicable, proceedings were added due to RS research focus.

Table A2. Identified Articles on Behavioral Biases in RSs

Author(s)	Research Field / Discipline	RS Dimension			Behavioral Bias			Data
		Quantity and Selection	Ranking	Explanation and Reviews	Preferences	Beliefs	Decision-Making	
Adomavicius et al. (2013)	Information Systems	x		x		x		lab
Adomavicius et al. (2019)	Information Systems			x		x		lab
Baum and Spann (2014)	Information Systems			x	x			lab
Bian et al. (2012)	Artificial Intelligence	x					x	obs
Bollen et al. (2010)	Recommender Systems	x	x				x	lab
Chernev (2003)	Marketing	x					x	lab
Collins et al. (2018)	Information Systems		x				x	field
Dandekar et al. (2013)	Multidisciplinary	x			x			na[6]
Deng and Chau (2021)	Information Systems			x			x	lab
Diehl (2005)	Marketing		x				x	lab
Eryarsoy and Piramuthu (2014)	Information Systems		x	x		x		lab
Gai and Klesse (2019)	Marketing			x	x		x	field

---

[6] This article was included due to the journal's high impact factor and citation count.

Guo et al. (2023)	Information Systems		x			x	x	lab
Häubl et al. (2010)	Marketing		x			x	x	lab
Ho et al. (2017)	Information Systems			x		x		obs
Köcher et al. (2019)	Marketing	x				x		field
Lee and Hosanagar (2014)	Information Systems	x			x			field
Lee and Hosanagar (2019)	Information Systems	x			x			field
Lerman and Hogg (2014)	Multidisciplinary		x				x	lab
Lill and Spann (2022)	Information Systems	x			x			field
Liu et al. (2016)	Recommender Systems			x	x			obs
Melchiorre et al. (2023)	Artificial Intelligence	x	x			x	x	obs
Mousavi et al. (2021)	Information Systems	x					x	lab
Murphy et al. (2006)	Information Systems		x				x	field
Rafai et al. (2022)	Marketing	x					x	field
Sánchez-Moreno et al. (2020)	Information Systems	x			x			obs
Schwind and Buder (2012)	Psychology	x				x		lab
Schwind et al. (2012)	Computer Science	x				x		lab
Su et al. (2023)	Psychology	x		x	x			obs

Tang and Wu (2022)	Information Systems	x				x		lab
Teppan and Zanker (2015)	Management	x	x				x	lab
Teppan et al. (2011)	Recommender Systems	x					x	lab
Ursu (2018)	Marketing		x				x	field
Wang and Wang (2014)	Computer Science			x	x			obs
Wei et al. (2022)	Information Systems	x			x			obs
Willemsen et al. (2016)	Computer Science	x					x	lab
Yalcin and Bilge (2022)	Information Systems	x			x			obs
Yang et al. (2013)	Multidisciplinary			x		x		obs
Yang et al. (2024)	Management			x			x	lab
Zhang (2011)	Recommender Systems			x		x		lab
Zhang et al. (2022)	Management	x		x			x	lab
Zhao et al. (2022)	Artificial Intelligence		x		x			obs
Zhou et al. (2023)	Information Systems	x		x	x			sim
Total		**24**	**12**	**15**	**14**	**13**	**20**	

Notes. Data and methodology: "lab" (laboratory experiment), "field" (field experiment), "obs" (secondary data analysis of observational data), "sim" (simulated data), "na" (not applicable)

References

Adomavicius G, Tuzhilin A (2005) Toward the next generation of recommender systems: A survey of the state-of-the-art and possible extensions. *IEEE transactions on knowledge and data engineering* 17(6):734-749.

Adomavicius G, Bockstedt J, Curley S, Zhang J (2019) Reducing recommender systems biases: An investigation of rating display designs. *MIS Quarterly* 43(4):19-18.

Adomavicius G, Bockstedt JC, Curley SP, Zhang J (2013) Do recommender systems manipulate consumer preferences? A study of anchoring effects. *Information Systems Research* 24(4):956-975.

Aggarwal CC (2016) *Recommender Systems* (Springer, Yorktown Heights, NY, USA).

Aivazoglou M, Roussos AO, Margaris D, Vassilakis C, Ioannidis S, Polakis J, Spiliotopoulos D (2020) A fine-grained social network recommender system. *Social Network Analysis and Mining* 10:1-18.

Bairathi M, Zhang X, Lambrecht A (2022) The value of platform endorsement. *Available at SSRN 4144605*.

Baum D, Spann M (2014) The interplay between online consumer reviews and recommender systems: An experimental analysis. *International journal of electronic commerce* 19(1):129-162.

Bettman JR, Luce MF, Payne JW (1998) Constructive consumer choice processes. *Journal of consumer research* 25(3):187-217.

Bian J, Dong A, He X, Reddy S, Chang Y (2012) User action interpretation for online content optimization. *IEEE transactions on knowledge and data engineering* 25(9):2161-2174.

Bless H, Schwarz N (2010) Mental construal and the emergence of assimilation and contrast effects: The inclusion/exclusion model. *Advances in Experimental Social Psychology*, vol. 42 (Elsevier), 319-373.

Bollen D, Knijnenburg BP, Willemsen MC, Graus M (2010) Understanding choice overload in recommender systems. *Proceedings of the fourth ACM Conference on Recommender Systems*, 63-70.

Boratto L, Fenu G, Marras M (2021) Connecting user and item perspectives in popularity debiasing for collaborative recommendation. *Information Processing & Management* 58(1):102387.

Charness G, Rabin M (2002) Understanding social preferences with simple tests. *The quarterly journal of economics* 117(3):817-869.

Chen J, Dong H, Wang X, Feng F, Wang M, He X (2023) Bias and debias in recommender system: A survey and future directions. *ACM Transactions on Information Systems* 41(3):1-39.

Chernev A (2003) When more is less and less is more: The role of ideal point availability and assortment in consumer choice. *Journal of consumer Research* 30(2):170-183.

Collins A, Tkaczyk D, Aizawa A, Beel J (2018) Position bias in recommender systems for digital libraries. *International Conference on Information* (Springer), 335-344.

Conlin M, O'Donoghue T, Vogelsang TJ (2007) Projection bias in catalog orders. *American Economic Review* 97(4):1217-1249.

Dandekar P, Goel A, Lee DT (2013) Biased assimilation, homophily, and the dynamics of polarization. *Proceedings of the National Academy of Sciences* 110(15):5791-5796.

DellaVigna S (2009) Psychology and economics: Evidence from the field. *Journal of Economic literature* 47(2):315-372.

Deng B, Chau M (2021) The Effect of Recommendation Framing on the Outcomes of Recommendation Agents. *Proceedings of the 25th Pacific Asia Conference on Information Systems*, 193.

Dewan S, Kim J, Nian T (2023) Economic Impacts of Platform-Endorsed Quality Certification: Evidence from Airbnb. *MIS Quarterly* 47(3).

Diehl K (2005) When two rights make a wrong: Searching too much in ordered environments. *Journal of Marketing Research* 42(3):313-322.

Dowling K, Guhl D, Klapper D, Spann M, Stich L, Yegoryan N (2020) Behavioral biases in marketing. *Journal of the Academy of Marketing Science* 48(3):449-477.

Eryarsoy E, Piramuthu S (2014) Experimental evaluation of sequential bias in online customer reviews. *Information & Management* 51(8):964-971.

Färber M, Coutinho M, Yuan S (2023) Biases in scholarly recommender systems: impact, prevalence, and mitigation. *Scientometrics* 128(5):2703-2736.

Farronato C, Fradkin A, MacKay A (2023) Self-preferencing at Amazon: evidence from search rankings. *AEA Papers and Proceedings* (American Economic Association 2014 Broadway, Suite 305, Nashville, TN 37203), 239-243.

Gai PJ, Klesse A-K (2019) Making recommendations more effective through framings: Impacts of user-versus item-based framings on recommendation click-throughs. *Journal of Marketing* 83(6):61-75.

Ge M, Delgado-Battenfeld C, Jannach D (2010) Beyond accuracy: evaluating recommender systems by coverage and serendipity. *Proceedings of the fourth ACM Conference on Recommender Systems*, 257-260.

Gomez-Uribe CA, Hunt N (2015) The netflix recommender system: Algorithms, business value, and innovation. *ACM Transactions on Management Information Systems (TMIS)* 6(4):1-19.

Gulsoy M, Yalcin E, Bilge A (2023) Robustness of privacy-preserving collaborative recommenders against popularity bias problem. *PeerJ Computer Science* 9:1438.

Guo X, Wang L, Zhang M, Chen G (2023) First things first? Order effects in online product recommender systems. *ACM Transactions on Computer-Human Interaction* 30(1):1-35.

Häubl G, Dellaert BGC, Donkers B (2010) Tunnel Vision: Local Behavioral Influences on Consumer Decisions in Product Search. *Marketing Science* 29(3):438-455.

Herings PJ-J, Rohde KI (2006) Time-inconsistent preferences in a general equilibrium model. *Economic Theory* 29:591-619.

Ho Y-C, Wu J, Tan Y (2017) Disconfirmation effect on online rating behavior: A structural model. *Information Systems Research* 28(3):626-642.

Huber J, Payne JW, Puto C (1982) Adding asymmetrically dominated alternatives: Violations of regularity and the similarity hypothesis. *Journal of Consumer Research* 9(1):90-98.

Jindal P (2015) Risk preferences and demand drivers of extended warranties. *Marketing Science* 34(1):39-58.

Kaminskas M, Bridge D (2016) Diversity, serendipity, novelty, and coverage: a survey and empirical analysis of beyond-accuracy objectives in recommender systems. *ACM Transactions on Interactive Intelligent Systems (TiiS)* 7(1):1-42.

Köcher S, Jugovac M, Jannach D, Holzmüller HH (2019) New hidden persuaders: an investigation of attribute-level anchoring effects of product recommendations. *Journal of Retailing* 95(1):24-41.

Kotkov D, Wang S, Veijalainen J (2016) A survey of serendipity in recommender systems. *Knowledge-Based Systems* 111:180-192.

Lerman K, Hogg T (2014) Leveraging position bias to improve peer recommendation. *PloS one* 9(6):e98914.

Levin IP, Schneider SL, Gaeth GJ (1998) All frames are not created equal: A typology and critical analysis of framing effects. *Organizational behavior and human decision processes* 76(2):149-188.

Li X, Grahl J, Hinz O (2022) How Do Recommender Systems Lead to Consumer Purchases? A Causal Mediation Analysis of a Field Experiment. *Information Systems Research* 33(2):620-637.

Lill M, Spann M (2022) Influence of Assimilation Effects on Recommender Systems. *Proceedings of the 43rd International Conference on Information Systems.*

Linden G, Smith B, York J (2003) Amazon.com recommendations: Item-to-item collaborative filtering. *IEEE Internet computing* 7(1):76-80.

Liu Y, Cao X, Yu Y (2016) Are you influenced by others when rating? Improve rating prediction by conformity modeling. *Proceedings of the 10th ACM conference on recommender systems,* 269-272.

Melchiorre AB, Penz D, Ganhör C, Lesota O, Fragoso V, Fritzl F, Parada-Cabaleiro E, Schubert F, Schedl M (2023) Emotion-aware music tower blocks (EmoMTB): an intelligent audiovisual interface for music discovery and recommendation. *International Journal of Multimedia Information Retrieval* 12(1):13.

Moore DA, Healy PJ (2008) The trouble with overconfidence. *Psychological review* 115(2):502.

Mousavi N, Bockstedt J, Adamopoulos P (2021) Personalization and the Decoy Effect. *Proceedings of the 42nd International Conference on Information Systems.*

Murphy J, Hofacker C, Mizerski R (2006) Primacy and recency effects on clicking behavior. *Journal of computer-mediated communication* 11(2):522-535.

Palmatier RW, Houston MB, Hulland J (2018) Review articles: purpose, process, and structure. *Journal of the Academy of Marketing Science* 46:1-5.

Pei C, Zhang Y, Zhang Y, Sun F, Lin X, Sun H, Wu J, Jiang P, Ge J, Ou W (2019) Personalized re-ranking for recommendation. *Proceedings of the 13th ACM Conference on Recommender Systems,* 3-11.

Piramuthu S, Kapoor G, Zhou W, Mauw S (2012) Input online review data and related bias in recommender systems. *Decision Support Systems* 53(3):418-424.

Rabin M (2002) A perspective on psychology and economics. *European economic review* 46(4-5):657-685.

Rafai I, Babutsidze Z, Delahaye T, Hanaki N, Acuna-Agost R (2022) No evidence of attraction effect among recommended options: A large-scale field experiment on an online flight aggregator. *Decision Support Systems* 153(113672):1-11.

Resnick P, Varian HR (1997) Recommender systems. *Communications of the ACM* 40(3):56-58.

Sánchez-Moreno D, López Batista V, Vicente MDM, Sánchez Lázaro ÁL, Moreno-García MN (2020) Exploiting the user social context to address neighborhood bias in collaborative filtering music recommender systems. *Information* 11(9):439.

Schedl M, Knees P, McFee B, Bogdanov D (2021) Music recommendation systems: Techniques, use cases, and challenges. *Recommender Systems Handbook*, vol. 3 (Springer), 927-971.

Schrader U, Hennig-Thurau T (2009) VHB-JOURQUAL2: method, results, and implications of the German academic association for business research's journal ranking. *Business Research* 2:180-204.

Schwind C, Buder J (2012) Reducing confirmation bias and evaluation bias: When are preference-inconsistent recommendations effective–and when not? *Computers in Human Behavior* 28(6):2280-2290.

Schwind C, Buder J, Cress U, Hesse FW (2012) Preference-inconsistent recommendations: An effective approach for reducing confirmation bias and stimulating divergent thinking? *Computers & Education* 58(2):787-796.

Simon HA (1955) A behavioral model of rational choice. *The quarterly journal of economics*:99-118.

Simonson I (1989) Choice based on reasons: The case of attraction and compromise effects. *Journal of Consumer Research* 16(2):158-174.

--- (2008) Will I like a "medium" pillow? Another look at constructed and inherent preferences. *Journal of Consumer Psychology* 18(3):155-169.

Smyth B, McClave P (2001) Similarity vs. Diversity. *Proceedings of the 4th International Conference on Case-Based Reasoning* (Springer), 347-361.

Su X, Li P, Zhu X (2023) The Influence of Herd Mentality on Rating Bias and Popularity Bias: A Bi-Process Debiasing Recommendation Model Based on Matrix Factorization. *Behavioral Sciences* 13(1):63.

Swaminathan V (2003) The Impact of Recommendation Agents on Consumer Evaluation and Choice: The Moderating Role of Category Risk, Product Complexity, and Consumer Knowledge. *Journal of Consumer Psychology* 13(1-2):93-101.

Tang M-C, Wu P-M (2022) Reconciling the effects of positive and negative electronic word of mouth: roles of confirmation bias and involvement. *Online Information Review* 46(1):114-133.

Teppan EC, Zanker M (2015) Decision Biases in Recommender Systems. *Journal of Internet Commerce* 14(2):255-275.

Teppan EC, Felfernig A, Isak K (2011) Decoy effects in financial service e-sales systems. *Proceedings of the Workshop Decisions@ RecSys, in Conjunction with the Fourth ACM Conference on Recommender Systems*, 1-8.

Ursu RM (2018) The power of rankings: Quantifying the effect of rankings on online consumer search and purchase decisions. *Marketing Science* 37(4):530-552.

Vargas S, Castells P (2011) Rank and Relevance in Novelty and Diversity Metrics for Recommender Systems. *Proceedings of the fifth ACM Conference on Recommender systems*, 109-116.

Wang T, Wang D (2014) Why Amazon's ratings might mislead you: The story of herding effects. *Big data* 2(4):196-204.

Wang W, Benbasat I (2007) Recommendation agents for electronic commerce: Effects of explanation facilities on trusting beliefs. *Journal of Management Information Systems* 23(4):217-246.

Wang Y, Ma W, Zhang M, Liu Y, Ma S (2023) A survey on the fairness of recommender systems. *ACM Transactions on Information Systems* 41(3):1-43.

Webster J, Watson RT (2002) Analyzing the past to prepare for the future: Writing a literature review. *MIS quarterly* 26(2):13-23.

Wei F, Chen S, Jin J, Zhang S, Zhou H, Wu Y (2022) Adaptive alleviation for popularity bias in recommender systems with knowledge graph. *Security and Communication Networks* 2022(1):4264489.

Willemsen MC, Graus MP, Knijnenburg BP (2016) Understanding the role of latent feature diversification on choice difficulty and satisfaction. *User Modeling and User-Adapted Interaction* 26:347-389.

Yalcin E, Bilge A (2022) Evaluating unfairness of popularity bias in recommender systems: A comprehensive user-centric analysis. *Information Processing & Management* 59(6):103100.

Yang Y, Zheng J, Yu Y, Qiu Y, Wang L (2024) The role of recommendation sources and attribute framing in online product recommendations. *Journal of Business Research* 174:114498.

Yang Z, Zhang Z-K, Zhou T (2013) Anchoring bias in online voting. *Europhysics Letters* 100(6):68002.

Zaizi FE, Qassimi S, Rakrak S (2023) Multi-objective optimization with recommender systems: A systematic review. *Information Systems*:102233.

Zhang J (2011) Anchoring effects of recommender systems. *Proceedings of the fifth ACM conference on Recommender systems*, 375-378.

Zhang J, Balaji M, Luo J, Jha S (2022) Effectiveness of product recommendation framing on online retail platforms. *Journal of Business Research* 153:185-197.

Zhang L (2013) The Definition of Novelty in Recommendation System. *Journal of Engineering Science & Technology Review* 6(3):141-145.

Zhao Z, Chen J, Zhou S, He X, Cao X, Zhang F, Wu W (2022) Popularity bias is not always evil: Disentangling benign and harmful bias for recommendation. *IEEE Transactions on Knowledge and Data Engineering*.

Zheng Y, Qin J, Wei P, Chen Z, Lin L (2023) CIPL: Counterfactual Interactive Policy Learning to Eliminate Popularity Bias for Online Recommendation. *IEEE Transactions on Neural Networks and Learning Systems*.

Zhou M, Zhang J, Adomavicius G (2023) Longitudinal impact of preference biases on recommender systems' performance. *Information Systems Research*.

Article 2:
Influence of Assimilation Effects on Recommender Systems[1]

Markus Lill   Martin Spann

Recommender systems (RSs) are a common approach in retail e-commerce to support consumers in finding relevant products. Not surprisingly, user acceptance of personalized product recommendations tends to be higher, leading to higher click rates. Since contextual information also influences user search behavior, we analyze the importance of similarity between recommendations and the underlying context a currently inspected product provides. Using data from a midsize European retail company, we conduct a field experiment and investigate the role of similarities between focal product information and recommendations from a collaborative filtering algorithm. We find that contextual similarity, primarily visual similarity contributes much explanation to consumer click behavior, underlining the importance of contextual and content information in the RS's environment.

Keywords: Recommender systems, assimilation-contrast theory, collaborative filtering, consumer behavior

---

[1] This article is based on the following paper: Lill, M., and Spann, M. (2022). Influence of Assimilation Effects on Recommender Systems. *Proceedings of the 43rd International Conference on Information Systems*, Copenhagen.

1   Introduction

Recommender systems (RSs) are an established tool in e-commerce that help users to find the right products. One of the primary purposes is filtering from a large set of available products down to a smaller subset of user-relevant products (Häubl and Trifts 2000). Extant research and industry practice in e-commerce has shown that this preselection mechanism significantly impacts the decision-making process of online users (Xiao and Benbasat 2007) and can lead to higher sales (Pathak et al. 2010). Providing suggestions that fit user preferences increases the chances that consumers accept and evaluate the preselected products (Hu and Pu 2009).

However, research goes beyond simple accuracy analyses of RSs and accounts for other metrics to evaluate the quality of recommendations, e.g., measuring the diversity or serendipity of recommendations (Bradley and Smyth 2001, Kaminskas and Bridge 2016). There is a broad consensus that surprising and diverse product suggestions further improve the quality and acceptance of RSs. While characteristics such as diversity and serendipity represent a view of RSs through analyzing the recommendations in a neutral environment, we contribute to the understanding of the influence of contextual information on RS effectiveness. More precisely, we want to understand what attributes of a recommendable item provide a context that affects the acceptance of recommendations. In particular, our results contest the usefulness of diverse and serendipitous recommendations in retail. Our results have important implications for RS design to increase click and conversion rates.

Our theoretical approach rests on the assumption that the acceptance of recommendations depends on the context in which they are presented and that the focal product that a user is currently inspecting provides an environmental context. Especially, we propose that congruence of recommendations and the information from products that a user most recently inspected impact the acceptance of suggested products. Therefore, we argue that recommendable items themselves already provide a context-rich environment to influence customer behavior. We apply the assimilation-contrast theory and predict that similarities across the context in which recommendations are provided to a consumer and the presence of a currently inspected product lead to the inclusion and acceptance of recommendations. As users navigate different product detail pages (PDPs), we find that visual overlap of the focal product and its recommendations leads to higher click rates. Similar products that share attributes with the focal product tend to positively impact users' click behavior. Even though content-based RSs have been tested to use image similarity (Addagarla and Amalanathan 2020), we suggest a more holistic view on RSs. By incorporating the RS's environment, we add to the understanding of recommendation quality and calculation. We provide insights that explain additional influences on the acceptance of recommendations.

2   Related Literature

Our paper is related to the literature on assimilation and contrast effects in social decision-making and collaborative filtering RSs, summarized below.

2.1   Assimilation and Contrast Effects in Recommender Systems

An important field of research is the influence of prior information on the decision-making process of individuals. Strack et al. (1985) have shown that information most salient to a user and provided prior to a decision influences this particular decision. A well-researched and established phenomenon is that other products are perceived as more valuable and interesting in the presence of less appealing offers. On the other hand, positive environments can wear off on the perception of products, and positive attributes of other products lead to better opinions.

However, contextual effects do not always have the same direction and can deviate between assimilation and contrast (Bless and Schwarz 2010). In order to achieve an assimilation effect (Sigall and Landy 1973), the context stimulus and the target stimulus must be mentally categorized into the same group by the consumer. This process also refers to the inclusion of the target into the context stimuli. Therefore, attributes of a currently inspected focal product can lead to an acceptance of recommended products that are provided on the same page. On the other hand, contrast effects (Kenrick and Gutierres 1980) are likely to occur when both stimuli are perceived as belonging to different categories. The focal product and recommendations are perceived as too far apart and assigned to different mental groups.

It requires cognitive resources to categorize context and target stimulus. As Bless and Schwarz (2010) pointed out, this categorization process is supported by levels of similarity. They show that the more similar target and context stimuli are, the more likely inclusion of the target stimuli and assimilation will occur. Furthermore, an objective threshold is not obtainable. Wänke (1998) also states that even a single shared attribute could lead to assimilation. In RSs research, assimilation effects are primarily known for product ratings. Amatriain et al. (2009) have shown that when sequentially providing products by a recommendation engine with comparable ratings, users are likely to give the same rating to preceding products like those discovered before. Furthermore, Köcher et al. (2019) have shown that users pay more attention to product alternatives that are similar to recommendations.

While there is a broad field of research discussing the various types of diversification (Kunaver and Požrl 2017) and serendipity (Kotkov et al. 2016) metrics in RSs, they all agree that both diversity and serendipity are favorable attributes of RSs that improve the user's perception and experience of RS utility. Kotkov et al. (2016) argue that product suggestions that are novel and substantially different from already discovered products improve overall user satisfaction and acceptance of RSs. Since we do not further analyze the differences between diversity and serendipity, we affirm that both metrics provide a reasonable contrast to already discovered products, more precisely to a currently inspected focal product.

Nonetheless, it has to be noted that the "Assimilation-Contrast" theory is still an under-researched area in RSs. Most studies focus on the influence of explicit ratings on customer choices and the evaluation of products (Masthoff and Gatt 2006, X. Zhang et al. 2017, Guo et al. 2022) whereas the influence of recommendable products on a list of recommendations requires further elaboration in research.

2.2   Collaborative Filtering

Collaborative filtering (CF) is an umbrella of methods in RSs utilizing implicit or explicit ratings from users to form recommendations. Implicit ratings could be derived from user behavior, e.g. page views or purchases, instead of explicit ratings, which a user actively specifies. In contrast to other RSs, like content-based methods, CF does not rely on product or user attributes. CF is a common and widely implemented approach in business practice and academic research (Lee and Hosanagar 2019, Li et al. 2022). The core concept of CF is to find similarities between users and products. In this paper, we focus on item-based CF, similar to the approach used by Amazon (Hardesty 2019).

An essential part of CF is the so-called rating matrix R which is a $m \times n$ ($m, n \in N$) matrix of m users and n products. Usually, in retail-based e-commerce shops, m is much larger than n. Each row r_i. represents all provided ratings of user i. It is expected that most entries r_{ij} of the rating matrix R are empty, resulting in a sparse matrix. Similarities are calculated across columns (products) in the item-based CF approach. Only the top $k \in N$ product-to-product connections with the highest similarity scores are kept and ordered descendingly. Therefore, the most similar item is recommended first. Different similarity measures are applicable, e.g. Pearson correlation and cosine similarity. However, when provided unary ratings, i.e., ratings that only account for positive feedback and cannot embrace dislikes, Jaccard distance is a possible similarity measure to calculate recommendations (Suganeshwari and Ibrahim 2018).

Note that the item-based CF approach has lower computational complexity because there are fewer similarities to calculate compared to the vast amount of different visiting users. Also, similarities across products remain robust when new ratings are provided. Therefore, item-based CF is considered to be more stable over time. Item-based recommendations are often perceived as more relevant since a user's own ratings are used to calculate similarities across products compared to user-based CF, which depends on ratings from other users who might have different interests. As such, recommendations are also perceived as less diverse and serendipitous than user-based CF approaches (Aggarwal 2016).

3   Data

3.1   Randomized Field Experiment

We use data from a medium-sized European retail company operating in the field of sports activities. The company has introduced a RS using an item-based CF algorithm utilizing the past-purchase behavior of customers. As shown by Li et al. (2022), a total of three recommendations are perceived as being an adequate number of recommendations. The respective product suggestions are displayed as a list on product detail pages (PDPs) directly below the product description. The recommended products are sorted in descending order according to the similarity obtained by the Jaccard Distance from the CF algorithm. A click on any listed product redirects the user to the respective PDP of the selected product. In order to reduce assimilation effects from recommendation framing (Gai and Klesse 2019) we kept the formulation, i.e., the presentation of products, neutral ("More products...").

We randomly split all visiting users based on their cookie ID, assigning each user to either a control or treatment group. Users from the treatment group received three recommendations on each PDP they visited based on the CF algorithm utilizing the focal product. Analogously to the treatment group, users from the control group also retrieved a list of three products on the PDPs. However, these products were drawn randomly from the set of all available products. We have chosen to provide random recommendations to capture variability among the displayed products in the control group. An alternative control algorithm, e.g. "bestselling" products, would display the same products on all PDPs.

We emphasize that the random recommendations in the control group do not represent a clear demarcation from the treatment effect. Since random product suggestions draw each product from the set of all available products with the same probability, selecting a product that the item-based CF model would recommend simply happens by chance. However, the probability of randomly selecting at least one product from the actual three product CF recommendations is low (2.27%).

Our data span 54 days and contain 13,041 observations from 4,451 users, with 2,217 users assigned to the treatment group and 2,234 users in the control group. Recommendations are drawn from a set of 394 products. 13 new products were introduced during the experiment, which led to products without available recommendations. Thereby, we removed those new articles from the treatment and control groups ensuring that treatment and control group users rely on an identical product base. Each observation represents a unique view of the product recommendations on a specific product's PDP by a user. We ensured that the recommendations were scrolled into view and displayed in the viewport of the user's device to make sure that the consumer could recognize all information. We also collected device information for each user to control for mobile and non-mobile (i.e., tablet, desktop) usage.

3.2   Descriptive Statistics

Table 1 describes the observed behavior data. The dependent variable *click* measures whether a user clicked on any of the three recommended products — *mobile* controls for different device usage. We introduced *mobile* since prior research suggests that click rates tend to be higher on mobile devices, e.g. through accidental clicks (Stewart et al. 2012). As shown in Table 1, 64.2% of recommendation views originate from mobile devices. Further investigation of the data set shows that 2,851 (64.1%) consumers use a mobile device, in line with the current mobile usage trend. Also, the number of mobile users among the control and treatment groups shows no significant difference, indicating a clean randomization procedure. Since our theoretical construct rests on the assumption that assimilation effects happen through the inclusion of recommendations into the context of a currently inspected product through levels of similarity, we need to define user-obtainable similarity metrics. Therefore, in order to measure similarities between the focal product and recommendations, we introduced three variables. We defined a variable *visual similarity* to measure the visual overlap between the focal product and its recommendations. We utilized the open-source Python "sentence-transformers" library by the Ubiquitous Knowledge Processing Lab [2], which provides pre-trained transformers. We then calculated the pairwise image similarities between the focal and each recommended product. The comparison accounts for the shape and color of the product images. The resulting similarity scores fall into the interval [0;1], with higher scores indicating visually closer images than lower scores. Afterward, we calculated the average pairwise similarity between focal and all recommended products.

Furthermore, we calculated *price similarity* as the inverse of the absolute difference between the focal product price and the mean price of the recommended products. In order to account for unrecognizable differences between prices, we have set minor price differences below 1 equal to 1. Finally, the variable *category similarity* measures the number of product recommendations that share at least one category with the focal product. We divided this number by 3 to obtain a measure between [0;1]. Product assignment to different categories had been executed by the marketing experts of the retail company.

---

[2] https://www.sbert.net/

Table 1. Descriptive Statistics

Variable	Mean	SD	Min	Max
Click	0.119	0.323	0	1
Mobile	0.642	0.480	0	1
Visual Similarity	0.314	0.251	0	0.940
Price Similarity	0.210	0.267	0.006	1
Category Similarity	0.258	0.316	0	1

Notes. Number of observations: 13,041

Correlation analysis of independent variables shows that the correlation between category and visual similarity is high (0.504) since products from the same category could share the same product branch, e.g. "jackets", "shirts & polos". However, note that products from the same category primarily represent similar usage purposes rather than visual similarities. The correlations between price and category similarity (0.242) and price and visual similarity (0.157) are relatively low.

We also grouped the dataset into treatment and control observations. We then calculated the intra-list diversity ILD (Ziegler et al. 2005, M. Zhang and Hurley 2008) as the average pairwise distance of the recommended products utilizing the similarity measures from above. Mean ILD scores for the control group are significantly higher than those for the treatment group. Therefore, the product recommendations in the control group show more diversity than those in the treatment group.

Figure 1. Click Rates

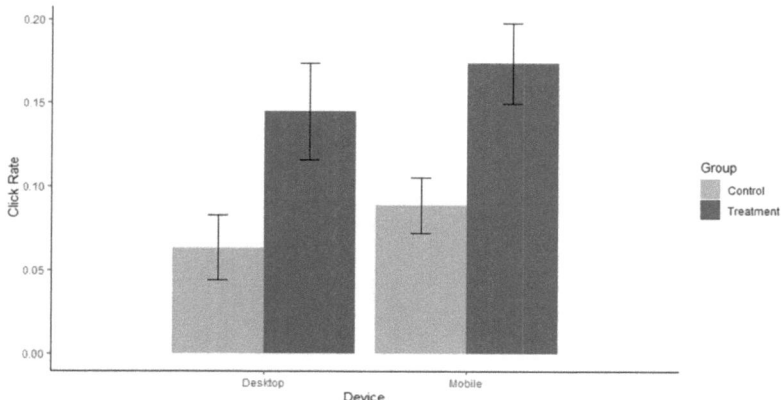

The overall click rate (i.e., click on any of the three recommended products) is 11.9%. Multiple views of the same product recommendations for a particular focal product are only counted once. Figure 1 depicts the average click rates differentiated by mobile and non-mobile usage for treatment and control groups, including 95% confidence intervals. The click rate for non-mobile users in the control group is 6.33%, and for the treatment group, it is 14.48%, compared to mobile users, with a click rate of 8.86% in the control group and 17.36% in the treatment group. The overall click rate in the control group is 7.99%, and in the treatment group, 16.28%, showing a significant difference between both groups ($\chi2 = 212.94$, p < 0.001). Therefore, we can assume that the users generally accept the recommendations in the treatment group.

4   Model and Results

Since we use panel data, we model users' click behavior through a logistic regression with random effects to account for heterogeneity across users. This model approach enables us to measure the influences of similarities independent of the different influences underlying basic user click rates. Our model looks as follows:

$$P(y_{it} = 1|x; \alpha_i) = \frac{1}{1 + exp(-(\alpha_i + \beta' x_{it}))}$$

(1)

$$i \in \{1, ..., m\}, t \in \{1, ..., T_i\}$$

where y_{it} is a binary variable whether the ith user has clicked on any of the presented recommended products at time point t. The term α_i captures part of the unobserved heterogeneity across different users and takes different values for each user in the sample. In order to compare our full random effects model (Model 3) for general acceptance of the recommendations, we estimate a random effects logistic regression with mobile and treatment as the only explanatory variables. Model 1 only includes the treatment effect (collaborative filtering recommendations vs. random recommendations) and mobile control variable. Model 2 adds the similarity variables: visual and price. Furthermore, Model 3 also includes category similarity. The usage of AIC test statistics shows that accounting for similarity measures improves the goodness of fit of our model. Model 2 and Model 3 show that visual similarity is positively related to a user's click probability, indicating a higher click rate on recommendations that are visually similar to the focal product. We explain this positive relationship by a higher degree of assimilation of the recommendations in the context of the focal product. Therefore, acceptance and a click on recommended products are higher when users perceive other products similar to the recently inspected product. Also, Model 3 shows a positive relationship between category similarity and click probability but only on a 5% significance level (p-value = 0.025). However, this might be due to the correlation between visual and category similarity, where visual overlap already partially explains the variance in category similarity. Also, note that category similarity only consists of four different values, whereas the other similarity measures are continuously defined on the interval [0;1]. Since we only accounted for shared categories across focal and recommended products, it is not possible to interpret category similarity as a closeness measure across different categories, e.g. the category "T-Shirts" might be closer to "Sportswear" as compared with "Accessories". Therefore, this lack of granularity on the category measure will not let us embrace the full potential of category similarity. Our data analysis cannot confirm that the general acceptance of recommendations depends on price congruence to the focal product.

Table 2. Estimation Results

Variable	*Model 1*	*Model 2*	*Model 3*
(Intercept)	-4.136*** (0.166)	-4.503*** (0.173)	-4.488*** (0.172)
Treatment	1.280*** (0.111)	0.870*** (0.118)	0.787*** (0.123)
Mobile	0.162 (0.110)	0.172 (0.110)	0.173 (0.110)
Visual Similarity		1.655*** (0.163)	1.538*** (0.171)
Price Similarity		-0.019 (0.137)	-0.066 (0.139)
Category Similarity			0.306** (0.137)
Observations	*13,041*	*13,041*	*13,041*
AIC	*8,000.1*	*7,897.4*	*7,894.5*

*p < 0.10, **p < 0.05, ***p < 0.01
Notes. Logistic regression models with user-specific random effects.

Model 2 and Model 3 do not show a significant influence of price similarity on click behavior. While this is surprising for purchase behavior, it is less surprising when analyzing acceptance behavior. Recall that we solely relied on a recommendation click rather than the actual purchase behavior. However, we do not argue that price is not an essential factor in the recommendation context.

We also estimated a fixed effects model as a robustness test, only accounting for similarity measures. Note that we cannot account for treatment and mobile usage in a fixed effects model since those are time-invariant variables that are already captured within the fixed effects terms. Additionally, we can only use data from users that show different values for y_{it} (Cameron and Miller 2015). Since many users never clicked on a recommendation, the total observations used dropped to 3,720. However, results show that visual similarity remains significant. A conservative interpretation is that visual similarity between a currently inspected product and its recommendations as a single significant, influential factor in RSs underlines the importance of recommendation context. The visual overlap of a focal product and the provided recommendations drive the click rate and, therefore, the acceptance of product suggestions. The inspectable attributes of a product already provide a context under which inclusion is likely to happen.

5   Limitations and Opportunities for Further Research

Our results are not without limitations. Due to our model setup, we could not incorporate newly released products. We argued that similarity provides a more significant explanatory part of click behavior than serendipity. We acknowledge that the serendipitous part of our RS is limited by model design. Especially since novelty is one of the factors driving serendipity, we must assume that our product recommendations might contain a less surprising factor. However, the number of new product introductions during the experiment was neglectable.

Furthermore, we only analyzed the acceptance of recommendations given a focal product on a PDP. This setting represents only a small part of e-commerce where recommendations can be shown to users. We need to assume that users generally show higher acceptance rates on PDPs as they navigate different detail pages to find the most suitable product. Therefore, acceptance of recommendations can only be assumed given a product context and not be generalized to recommendations that draw a user's first attention e.g. on an e-commerce homepage. Finally, an often-heard and well-known argument in RSs research is the lack of reproducibility of results. Since we only provided a single study in apparel retail e-commerce, we underline that the results from this paper stem from one particular retailer. Further research is needed to provide more evidence and analyze the transferability to other business branches.

However, we emphasize that our approach enables multiple directions for analyzing customer decision-making under RSs. Since we only investigated the comparison between a focal product and all of its recommendations, we did not answer which particular recommended product the user selected. We only modeled the acceptance of any recommended product from the list of recommendations. In line with the assimilation and contrast effects framework, we suggest that further analysis of the consistency or variation within the recommendations could give insights into the actual user selection behavior. Although we suggest that similarity is an essential driver for general recommendation acceptance, the literature suggests that accounting diversity within recommendations can significantly improve the quality of RSs (Kwon 2008). An embracing theory and further analysis could show that diversity matters only among recommendations but not across context and recommendations. As we account for heterogeneity across users, the assumption that similarity leads to higher acceptance of recommendations holds for both the treatment and the control group. Therefore, an extended analysis of the acceptance of random recommendations is also of particular interest since we can create more understanding of the selection behavior of users and the accuracy of RSs when we compare the accepted suggested products with personalized recommendations. Also closely related to user click behavior is the analysis of forming consideration sets. Incorporating contextual influences could also provide additional insights into the ongoing debate on whether RSs increase or decrease consideration set sizes (Goodman et al. 2013).

6   Conclusion and Next Steps

RSs provide personalized navigation elements which allow users to explore additional products. In retail e-commerce, they filter many available products down to a manageable number of products that can be displayed within the context of other products.

We add evidence from a field experiment that enables measuring the influence of contextual attributes on the interaction between a user and product recommendations. We show that, either using a RS or random product suggestions, the user acceptance of these suggestions can be partially explained by similarities between a focal product (that the user is currently inspecting) and the provided product suggestions. More precisely, we find that visual similarity between the products significantly influences users' click behavior. The more alike focal product and product suggestion images are, the more likely a click is performed. We explain this user behavior through the inclusion of product suggestions into the focal product context and the assimilation of attributes from the focal product to attributes of the suggested products. This influence remains significant without the presence of a RS, e.g. when suggested products are drawn randomly from the set of available products. In contrast to current research, we show that diversity becomes a less important attribute of RSs, given the presence of a focal product.

One practical key implication for companies is that in retail e-commerce, similarity across products seems to be more important to users than diversity. While we accounted for heterogeneity among users, we found that users generally prefer to accept visually similar products. This information can be incorporated into existing RSs through e.g. hybrid recommenders. For retailers, our findings imply that serendipitous product suggestions on product detail pages seem less helpful for users and lead to lower acceptance rates of recommendations.

To complete our paper, we will extend our framework and apply it to the concept of consideration sets. We will analyze the impact of assimilation effects in RSs in a more general view and evaluate the influences on the amount and type of products a user considers. Furthermore, we will use insights from consideration set analysis to observe changes in the customer purchase decision process and provide a complete view of the customer journey. We want to contribute to understanding how RSs lead to higher revenues. Therefore, we will also be able to study the long-term effects of diversity on customer behavior. Since we focused on click rates, we only checked the influences in the direct proximity of a user. In addition, we will extend data collection and gather more detailed information on user behavior and product details as well as conduct additional experiments that keep the general CF mechanism common but manipulate the similarity between the focal and the recommended products.

References

Addagarla SK, Amalanathan A (2020) Probabilistic unsupervised machine learning approach for a similar image recommender system for E-commerce. *Symmetry* 12(11):1783.

Aggarwal CC (2016) *Recommender Systems* (Springer, Yorktown Heights, NY, USA).

Amatriain X, Pujol JM, Oliver N (2009) I like it... i like it not: Evaluating user ratings noise in recommender systems. *International Conference on User Modeling, Adaptation, and Personalization* (Springer), 247-258.

Bless H, Schwarz N (2010) Mental construal and the emergence of assimilation and contrast effects: The inclusion/exclusion model. *Advances in Experimental Social Psychology*, vol. 42 (Elsevier), 319-373.

Bradley K, Smyth B (2001) Improving recommendation diversity. *Proceedings of the Twelfth Irish Conference on Artificial Intelligence and Cognitive Science* (Citeseer), 141-152.

Cameron AC, Miller DL (2015) A practitioner's guide to cluster-robust inference. *Journal of human resources* 50(2):317-372.

Gai PJ, Klesse A-K (2019) Making recommendations more effective through framings: Impacts of user-versus item-based framings on recommendation click-throughs. *Journal of Marketing* 83(6):61-75.

Goodman JK, Broniarczyk SM, Griffin JG, McAlister L (2013) Help or hinder? When recommendation signage expands consideration sets and heightens decision difficulty. *Journal of Consumer Psychology* 23(2):165-174.

Guo X, Wang Y, Huang L, Li J (2022) Assimilation and Contrast: The Two-sided Anchoring Effects of Recommender Systems. *Journal of Systems Science and Systems Engineering* 31(4):395-413.

Hardesty L (2019) The history of Amazon's recommendation algorithm, Collaborative filtering and beyond. *Amazon Science, available at https://www.amazon.science/the-history-of-amazons-recommendation-algorithm*.

Häubl G, Trifts V (2000) Consumer decision making in online shopping environments: The effects of interactive decision aids. *Marketing Science* 19(1):4-21.

Hu R, Pu P (2009) Acceptance issues of personality-based recommender systems. *Proceedings of the third ACM Conference on Recommender systems*, 221-224.

Kaminskas M, Bridge D (2016) Diversity, serendipity, novelty, and coverage: a survey and empirical analysis of beyond-accuracy objectives in recommender systems. *ACM Transactions on Interactive Intelligent Systems (TiiS)* 7(1):1-42.

Kenrick DT, Gutierres SE (1980) Contrast effects and judgments of physical attractiveness: When beauty becomes a social problem. *Journal of Personality and Social Psychology* 38(1):131.

Köcher S, Jugovac M, Jannach D, Holzmüller HH (2019) New Hidden Persuaders: An Investigation of Attribute-Level Anchoring Effects of Product Recommendations. *Journal of Retailing* 95(1):24-41.

Kotkov D, Wang S, Veijalainen J (2016) A survey of serendipity in recommender systems. *Knowledge-Based Systems* 111:180-192.

Kunaver M, Požrl T (2017) Diversity in recommender systems–A survey. *Knowledge-Based Systems* 123:154-162.

Kwon Y (2008) Improving top-n recommendation techniques using rating variance. *Proceedings of the 2008 ACM Conference on Recommender Systems*, 307-310.

Lee D, Hosanagar K (2019) How do recommender systems affect sales diversity? A cross-category investigation via randomized field experiment. *Information Systems Research* 30(1):239-259.

Li X, Grahl J, Hinz O (2022) How Do Recommender Systems Lead to Consumer Purchases? A Causal Mediation Analysis of a Field Experiment. *Information Systems Research* 33(2):620-637.

Masthoff J, Gatt A (2006) In pursuit of satisfaction and the prevention of embarrassment: affective state in group recommender systems. *User Modeling and User-Adapted Interaction* 16(3):281-319.

Pathak B, Garfinkel R, Gopal RD, Venkatesan R, Yin F (2010) Empirical analysis of the impact of recommender systems on sales. *Journal of Management Information Systems* 27(2):159-188.

Sigall H, Landy D (1973) Radiating beauty: effects of having a physically attractive partner on person perception. *Journal of Personality and Social Psychology* 28(2):218.

Stewart C, Hoggan E, Haverinen L, Salamin H, Jacucci G (2012) An Exploration of Inadvertent Variations in Mobile Pressure Input. *Proceedings of the 14th International Conference on Human-Computer Interaction with Mobile Devices and Services*, 35-38.

Strack F, Schwarz N, Gschneidinger E (1985) Happiness and Reminiscing: The Role of Time Perspective, Affect, and Mode of Thinking. *Journal of Personality and Social Psychology* 49(6):1460.

Suganeshwari G, Ibrahim SS (2018) A Comparison Study on Similarity Measures in Collaborative Filtering Algorithms for Movie Recommendation. *International Journal of Pure and Applied Mathematics* 119(15):1495-1505.

Wänke M (1998) Markenmanagement als Kategorisierungsproblem. *Zeitschrift für Sozialpsychologie* 29:117-123.

Xiao B, Benbasat I (2007) E-commerce Product Recommendation Agents: Use, Characteristics, and Impact. *MIS Quarterly* 31(1):137-209.

Zhang M, Hurley N (2008) Avoiding Monotony: Improving the Diversity of Recommendation Lists. *Proceedings of the 2008 ACM Conference on Recommender Systems*, 123-130.

Zhang X, Zhao J, Lui JC (2017) Modeling the Assimilation-Contrast Effects in Online Product Rating Systems: Debiasing and Recommendations. *Proceedings of the Eleventh ACM Conference on Recommender Systems*, 98-106.

Ziegler C-N, McNee SM, Konstan JA, Lausen G (2005) Improving Recommendation Lists Through Topic Diversification. *Proceedings of the 14th International Conference on World Wide Web*, 22-32.

Article 3:
Position and Contrast Effects in Recommender Systems[1]

Markus Lill   Martin Spann

This study examines how position and contrast effects influence user decision-making within recommender systems (RSs). Since these effects can induce behavioral biases that impact consumer choices, understanding their influence on RS effectiveness is crucial. Utilizing a field experiment, we analyze how recommendation placement and contrasts affect user acceptance rates. Our findings reveal that both the position of a focal item and its distinction from contrasting products significantly enhance click-through rates (CTRs). Greater visual differences between the focal item and other recommendations, as well as contrast with previously encountered items, increase CTRs, indicating that users are more likely to engage with recommendations that stand out. Our results challenge the assumption that the highest position in a recommendation list is always the most beneficial, showing that lower positions can lead to higher CTRs. This study provides valuable insights for optimizing RS design, emphasizing the importance of strategic placement and diversity to improve decision outcomes.

Keywords: Recommender systems, consumer behavior, behavioral biases, position bias, contrast effects

---

[1] This article is based on the following paper: Lill, M. and Spann, M. (2024). Position and Contrast Effects in Recommender Systems. *Working Paper, LMU Munich.*

1   Introduction

The advent and rapid development of digital technologies have transformed the e-commerce landscape, adding complex layers to consumer behavior and decision-making processes. A key component of this digital transformation has been the emergence of recommender systems (RSs). These systems utilize consumer data and predictive algorithms to suggest products or services tailored to individual preferences, enhancing the personalization of user experiences. The application of RS on digital platforms has become an integral part of retailers from various professions, including music and video streaming media (Gomez-Uribe and Hunt 2015, Schedl et al. 2021), social networks (Aivazoglou et al. 2020), news platforms (Schmalenbach et al. 2022), or marketplaces (Linden et al. 2003), applying RSs to guide consumers through the vast product or content catalog of digital platforms (Häubl and Trifts 2000). Understanding the mechanisms behind these systems is crucial, as effective recommendations can significantly enhance user satisfaction and business outcomes.

However, the ability of RSs to accurately predict the recommendations most likely to be chosen by users can be compromised by behavioral biases (Piramuthu et al. 2012). Consumer interactions with the RS are fed back into the RS, which can reinforce and amplify biases such as position bias (Ursu 2018) and contrast effects (Bless and Schwarz 2010) in user decision-making. These biases can distort the recommendations generated, leading to suboptimal user outcomes.

Position bias refers to the tendency of consumers to favor items based on their placement within a list rather than their product characteristics. This bias is often observed as a higher CTR for items appearing at the top of the recommendation list, potentially distorting items' perceived popularity and relevance. However, research also suggests that positions other than the first can be more beneficial for user acceptance, likely due to contrast effects (Häubl et al. 2010, Guo et al. 2023). Contrast effects occur when the differences in attractiveness between a focal product and surrounding items influence consumer choices (Bless and Schwarz 2010), often enhancing the appeal of the focal product.

A lot of current research has primarily focused on optimizing algorithms to improve CTRs of recommendations. Studies have extensively documented the impact of position bias, demonstrating that items placed higher in a list receive disproportionately more attention and clicks (Collins et al. 2018). However, literature on the role of contrast effects in RSs remains sparse, particularly in understanding how these effects can be strategically utilized to enhance user engagement.

Our motivation for this study stems from the need to bridge this gap in the existing literature and provide additional insights on contrast effects in RSs. We aim to explore how position and contrast effects can induce biases that influence user behavior in RSs. Specifically, we address how varying the position and contrast of recommendations affects the CTRs and overall user engagement in RSs.

This paper aims to contribute to the understanding of these dynamics by conducting a randomized field experiment that investigates the interplay between position bias and recommendation contrast. By examining the effects in our study, we seek to provide insights that can inform the design of more effective and equitable RSs.

2   Related Literature

Our paper is related to the literature on position bias in RS and contrast effects in consumer decision-making, which is summarized below.

2.1   Position Bias in Recommender Systems

Position bias refers to systematic deviations in user behavior influenced by the position of items, also known as *recommendation rankings*, rather than the intrinsic qualities of the items themselves (Collins et al. 2018). This bias manifests when users disproportionately favor items in certain positions due to cognitive shortcuts and perceptual tendencies. While high rankings generally reduce consumer search costs (Ursu 2018), they also lead to skewed decision-making, where users favor items regardless of their actual relevance or quality.

High rankings are critical in influencing user decisions. Studies have consistently shown that users are more likely to select items positioned at the top of a list. This can attributed to the *primacy effect* (Murphy et al. 2006), where individuals tend to remember and prioritize the first items they encounter. For instance, Collins et al. (2018) conducted a field experiment showing that recommendations at the top are clicked more often regardless of their fit, with the CTR of top positions being significantly higher. Similarly, Lerman and Hogg (2014) demonstrated in a lab experiment that items at the beginning of a list receive five times higher click rates independent of their appeal, attributing this to higher visibility and ease of discovery. Ursu (2018) also noted that highly ranked items are more visible and relevant, increasing their CTRs. Teppan and Zanker (2015) argue that primacy effects are especially pronounced when users need to invest more effort into considering their choices.

Conversely, items with low rankings may benefit from the *recency effect* (Murphy et al. 2006), where users give more importance to the last items they encounter. However, this effect is generally less pronounced than the primacy effect. Teppan and Zanker (2015) noted the presence of recency effects in their study but emphasized that the primacy effect was more dominant in e-commerce contexts (Granka et al. 2004, Felfernig et al. 2007). This suggests that while low-ranked items can sometimes benefit from being at the end of a list, their overall impact on user choice is limited compared to items at the top.

In contrast to positions at the beginning or end of a list, items neither at the top nor the end can benefit from the effects of comparative evaluation. Häubl et al. (2010) found that positioning items in the middle of a list could influence user perception through comparative evaluation with previously encountered items. This effect means that users are more likely to compare and evaluate items against their preceding neighbors, which can affect the overall decision-making process. Guo et al. (2023) provided additional insights, showing that placing the most relevant recommendation in the second position can enhance product comparison and lead to better decision outcomes and higher CTRs. They argue that comparison between items drives acceptance, and strategically placing items can optimize this process.

Position bias can result in "feedback loops," amplifying these effects in RSs (Krauth et al. 2022). When users consistently select items from higher positions, these items gain more visibility and user interaction data, reinforcing their top-ranked status and perpetuating the cycle of bias. This phenomenon, also known as *popularity bias* (Zhou et al. 2023), is well-documented in the literature. Initial position biases can lead to increased visibility and selection of certain items, skewing future recommendations and user behavior.

2.2   Contrast Effects in Consumer Decision Making

Contrast effects in consumer decision-making (Kenrick and Gutierres 1980) refer to how the perception of a product or service (*target stimulus*) can be influenced by comparing it with another product or service (*context stimulus*). This phenomenon is driven by the salience of information available to the consumer, significantly affecting decision-making processes (Strack et al. 1985). The presence of information displayed along with the decision object influences the decision: a concept known as contextual effects (Bless and Schwarz 2010). Depending on the specific context and stimuli, these effects can manifest as assimilation or contrast. Minimizing the shared characteristics between the target and context stimuli enhances the likelihood of contrast effects, ensuring that consumers distinctly perceive the differences between the options.

Contrast effects are especially helpful in marketing and retail strategies where businesses aim to influence consumer choices and perceptions (Bless and Schwarz 2010). Marketers can make the target product appear more appealing by strategically placing a product alongside higher-priced or lower-quality alternatives (Strack et al. 1985). This tactic leverages the contrast between the products, making the target product stand out favorably. For instance, displaying a moderately priced item next to an expensive one can make the former seem like a better value, encouraging consumers to choose it. Similarly, placing a high-quality product next to a lower-quality option can highlight its superior attributes, justifying its higher price. This approach influences consumer perception and can drive higher sales and enhance customer satisfaction by guiding them toward more favorable decisions (Bless and Schwarz 2010).

Furthermore, the concept of *local contrast* (Häubl et al. 2010) posits that consumers tend to overreact to the differences in attractiveness between the products they have inspected previously and the product they are currently considering. Through two field experiments, Häubl et al. (2010) demonstrate that local contrast significantly influences consumers' acceptance of products and their decision to stop searching for alternatives. Their findings suggest that when a currently viewed product stands out against previously viewed options, it appears more attractive to consumers, increasing its likelihood of being chosen. Similarly, the findings by Guo et al. (2023) also show that previously encountered products can enhance the acceptance rate of a currently inspected item. Their research extends the understanding of contrast effects by illustrating that placing the most relevant recommendation in the second position can facilitate better comparisons, leading to higher acceptance rates. This strategic placement allows users to make more informed decisions by comparing them in contrast to other recommendations.

3   Conceptual Framework

We develop a conceptual framework and a set of hypotheses to guide our analysis of the influence of position bias and contrast effects on user choice.

3.1   Context and Application in E-Commerce

Retailers typically use e-commerce platforms to sell products and enhance customer experience through personalized recommendations. In a typical online shopping environment, users often receive multiple recommendations on a product detail page (PDP) for a specific item, which we refer to as the *base product* or *base item*. The respective recommendations are typically displayed below the base product on the PDP, where users can discover additional items that may interest them. Primarily, recommendations are listed in product carousels, i.e., in a horizontal order. Typically, users browse the recommendations by inspecting the products from left to right by scrolling horizontally. We refer to items at the beginning of a recommendations list as *higher-ranked* items and those further to the end of the list as *lower-ranked* items.

There may be a need to highlight a specific product within this recommendation list. This specific item could be a product on sale that the e-commerce retailer wants to highlight, a new arrival that the retailer wants to promote, or a product that the retailer wants to clear out of inventory. Regardless of the overall click rate, retailers can draw more attention by strategically positioning these highlighted products within the recommendation carousel, potentially increasing CTRs and conversions. Therefore, we are interested in the choice of a specific highlighted recommendation. Following Häubl et al. (2010), we refer to this highlighted product as the *focal item*. The other recommendations presented in the list are referred to as *contrasting items*.

Figure 1. Conceptualization of Focal Item Position Effect and Recommendation Contrast[2]

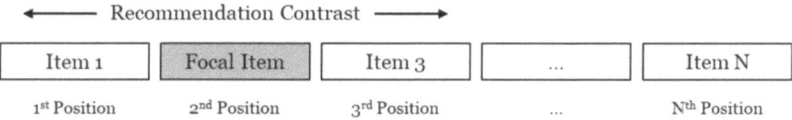

Our conceptual framework rests on the following main elements (see Figure 1). First, we are interested in the potential effects induced by the position of the focal item, the *focal item position effect*. Second, we want to analyze the impact of *recommendation contrast*, i.e., the contrast between the focal item and its contrasting items, on the CTR of the focal item and which dimensions potentially induce the contrast effect. These elements are crucial to understand how different recommendations interact with each other and influence user decisions.

3.2   Hypotheses Formulation

We formulate a set of hypotheses to guide our investigation into the influence of focal item position effects and recommendation contrast between a focal item and its contrasting items on user engagement.

Turning to focal item position effects, previous research has shown that positions other than the first in a list of recommendations can increase user acceptance. Häubl et al. (2010) demonstrated that users' perception of an item is highly influenced by its position, with a local contrast effect where previously inspected items affect the perception of the current item. Guo et al. (2023) found that placing the most relevant recommendation in the second position enhances user acceptance, as it allows for meaningful comparisons.

---

[2] Focal item on second position for illustration purposes. Placement of focal item can vary between any of the positions from first to last.

When the focal item is not the first product a user encounters, they are more likely to accept the recommendation. This effect is mainly driven by the opportunity to compare the focal item with previously encountered products, making the decision process more informed.

We also expect primacy effects (Murphy et al. 2006) to be less pronounced than the position effect induced by lower rankings. This contradicts findings that higher rankings result in the highest CTRs (Lerman and Hogg 2014, Collins et al. 2018, Ursu 2018). While the primacy effect suggests that users tend to remember and choose items presented first, we expect that the ability to compare the focal item with previously viewed items will mitigate this effect, leading to higher CTRs when the focal item is not the first in the list. However, Teppan and Zanker (2015) could not consistently find significant confirmation for primacy effects, making it reasonable to assume that lower rankings might be more effective in increasing CTRs.

Hypothesis 1:   *The CTR for the focal item is higher when it is in positions following the first in a list of recommendations.*

Turning to contrast effects, we measure recommendation contrast as the degree of difference between the focal product and the contrasting products. A higher recommendation contrast indicates higher differences between the product characteristics.

Contrast effects can occur when the focal recommendation is distinct from the surrounding context, specifically the contrasting products (Bless and Schwarz 2010).

Building on the work of Häubl et al. (2010) and Guo et al. (2023), we extend the concept of recommendation ranking by deliberately incorporating contrast. This involves analyzing the influence of non-relevant contrasting recommendations alongside the focal product to create a more pronounced difference. Such contrast makes the focal product stand out, enhancing its perceived value and increasing the CTR.

When the focal product significantly differs from the contrasting recommendations regarding visual appearance, price, or category, it stands out more to the user due to contrast effects (Bless and Schwarz 2010). This increased distinctiveness makes the focal product more noticeable and likely to attract clicks.

Hypothesis 2: *The CTR on the focal item increases with the contrast between the focal product and the other/contrasting recommendations.*

Furthermore, non-relevant recommendations can amplify the contrast effect, making the focal product more appealing. This technique is effective in research and practical applications to increase the CTR of specific products (Rafai et al. 2022). This heightened contrast makes the focal product appear more relevant and attractive. The enhanced disparity emphasizes the focal product's unique attributes, increasing its chances of being selected by the user.

Hypothesis 3: *Non-relevant contrasting recommendations amplify the positive contrast effect on the CTR on the focal product.*

4 Randomized Field Experiment

To test our hypotheses, we designed a randomized field experiment. This approach allows us to observe user interactions with RSs in a realistic setting, providing robust insights into the influence of focal item position effects and recommendation contrast on user choice.

4.1 Study Design

The experiment was conducted in collaboration with a European retail company specializing in sports apparel products. The RS utilized in this study was an item-based collaborative filtering (IBCF) algorithm (Linden et al. 2003) based on previous purchase data. Users were presented with three product recommendations on the product detail pages (PDPs). Li et al. (2022) demonstrated that three recommendations are perceived as an adequate number for users in a research setting. Also, in order to generate contrast effects, the size of the comparable products should not be too large (Bless and Schwarz 2010). Clicking any recommendation redirected the user to the selected product's detail page. The recommendations were presented with neutral framing ("More products…"), ensuring that the way the recommendations were displayed did not influence user perception or choice (Gai and Klesse 2019). This study design allows us to test our hypotheses.

The study design randomly assigns users into two groups based on their cookie IDs. The lifetime of a cookie was set to six months. Therefore, we ensure that each user is assigned to only one of the groups. Users in Group 1 received the three most relevant recommendations from the IBCF algorithm (illustrated in Figure 2). "Most relevant" in this case, refers to the three products with the highest IBCF ranking metrics with regard to the base product.

Figure 2. Example Recommendations for Group 1 (Three Highest Ranked IBCF Items) with the Focal Item on Position Three (Left: Desktop, Right: Mobile)

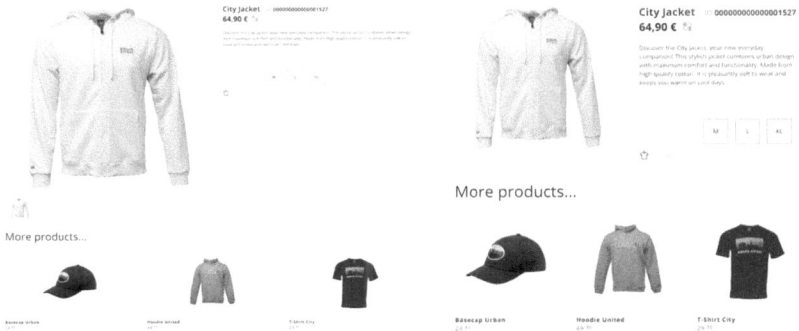

In contrast, users in Group 2 also received the most relevant recommendation, similar to Group 1. However, instead of the second and third most relevant recommendations, they received two random products from the lower tail of the total list of recommendations for a specific base product, as shown in Figure 3. The lower tail of recommendations is defined as the products that received the lowest IBCF rank for the focal product, indicating a potential low fit with the user's preferences. These items were selected to introduce a high level of contrast with the focal product, allowing us to observe the effects of recommendation contrast on user engagement. Instead of consistently choosing the same two least-fitting recommendations, we randomly selected products to ensure variability between the focal item and the other two products.

Figure 3. Example Recommendations for Group 2 (Highest IBCF Ranked Item plus two Non-Relevant Items) with the Focal Item on Position Three (Left: Desktop, Right: Mobile)

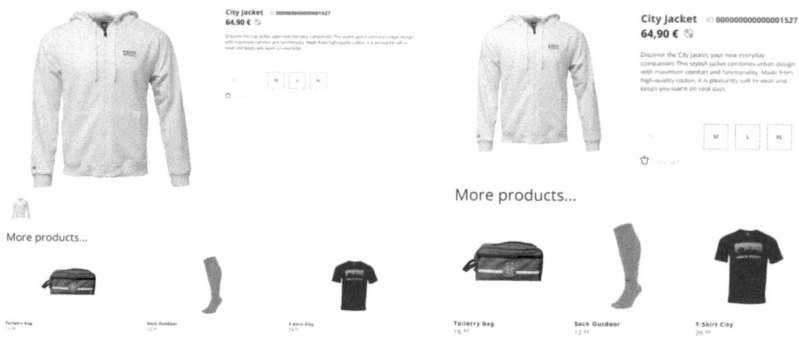

The positions of all recommendations were shuffled for each request. Therefore, the focal product also rotated positions from one to three. This shuffling allowed us to analyze position effects by observing user interactions across different positions for the focal product. By varying the placement of the focal product, we could assess how its position influences the CTR and overall user engagement. Additionally, to control for potential position effects, the randomization of product positions ensures that the observed effects are attributable to the position of the focal product and not to other confounding factors. This methodological approach allows for a robust analysis of focal item position effects and recommendation contrast. Table 1 summarizes the experimental design.

Table 1. Experimental Design

Experimental Group	**1**	**2**
Focal Recommendation	Highest IBCF rank	Highest IBCF rank
Contrasting Recommendations	2nd / 3rd highest IBCF rank	Low IBCF rank[a]
Position of recommendations	Randomized	Randomized

Notes. [a] Random selection of two products from the lower IBCF rank tail.

Each observation in the dataset represents a user view of the recommendation carousel. We ensured that the entire list of recommendations was displayed within the viewport of the user's device, verifying that the user could recognize all relevant product details such as name, price, and image. Whether a click on a desktop or a tap on mobile devices, a click on any recommendation resulted in a click event that captured the clicked position. By tracking the ranking of each recommendation position, we could distinguish whether the focal recommendation or one of the contrasting recommendations was selected. Additionally, we collected information on the device type, differentiating between mobile and desktop users.

4.2   Contrast Metrics

We calculate three distinct contrast measures to quantify the contrast between the focal product and its contrasting recommendations (for similar measures of contrast cf. Lill and Spann (2022)). The first measure assesses *visual contrast*, capturing differences in appearance such as color, shape, and overall design. The second measure evaluates *price contrast*, considering the disparity in cost between the focal product and its counterparts. The third measure examines *categorical contrast*, identifying differences in product categories to determine how distinct the focal product is from the accompanying recommendations.

We developed the *visual contrast* variable to quantify the visual difference between the focal product and its recommendations. We calculated the pairwise image contrast between the focal product and each recommended contrasting item using the open-source Python library "sentence-transformers" from the Ubiquitous Knowledge Processing Lab [3], which offers pre-trained transformers. This comparison considered the shape and color of the product images. The resulting contrast scores ranged from zero to one, with higher scores indicating greater visual contrast. We then computed the average pairwise contrast between the focal product and all recommended items.

Additionally, we calculated *price contrast* as one minus the inverse of the absolute difference between the focal product's price and the average price of the contrasting products. To account for negligible price differences, we set minor differences below one equal to zero. See equation (1) for the detailed calculation.

(1)
$$C := \begin{cases} 0 \ if \ |P_f - \bar{P}_r| < 1 \\ 1 - |P_f - \bar{P}_r|^{-1} \ otherwise \end{cases}$$
$$P_f = Focal \ Item \ Price$$
$$\bar{P}_r = Average \ Contrasting \ Item \ Price$$

This approach ensures that only significant price differences contribute to the contrast effect, while minor price variations are negligible.

Finally, we introduced *category contrast*. We measured the proportion of contrasting products that shared at least one category with the focal product. This

---

[3] https://www.sbert.net/

measure was standardized from zero to one by dividing the count by three. The result was subtracted from one. The retail company's marketing experts determined product category assignments.

4.3   Descriptive Statistics

The observation period for the study spanned 14 weeks, during which we collected 26,973 observations. The sample consisted of 8,751 users, with 4,327 users in Group 1 and 4,424 users in Group 2; however, the difference between groups is not significant (χ^2-value = 1.074, p-value = 0.300). 239 products were involved in the study, of which 222 contained recommendations. 19 new articles introduced during the observation period are not included in the analysis. Additionally, the recommendations were not recalculated during the study, ensuring consistency in the recommendations presented to users throughout the observation period.

51.42% of our observations fall within the treated Group 2, which received two non-relevant contrasting items. Further investigation shows that, on average, the number of observations for users in Group 1 is 3.01, while for users in Group 2 it is 3.12. Even though the difference is not significant (t-test value = 0.810, p-value = 0.417), the discrepancy can be attributed to the higher search costs experienced by users in Group 2. This may be explained by the presence of non-relevant recommendations, which may induce users to browse more products to find suitable ones, resulting in higher search costs.

The overall click rate is 11.05%, divided into 5.48% CTR for the focal recommendation and 5.57% for clicks on the contrasting recommendations. Therefore, nearly half of the clicks are contributed to the focal item. Table 2 provides an overview of user click behavior between the groups.

Table 2. Descriptive Statistics, Overall Comparison Between Groups

	Mean	
Click-Through Rate	*Group 1*	*Group 2*
Any Item [a]	0.117	0.104
Focal Item	0.052	0.057
Contrasting Item [b]	0.065	0.047

Notes. Number of observations 26,973. [a] CTR any item refers to click on any displayed item from the recommendation list. [b] CTR contrasting item refers to click on a non-focal item.

Mobile usage accounts for 60.6% of the interactions, which aligns with current mobile usage trends. The CTRs on mobile devices are significantly higher at 11.64%, compared to 10.01% on desktops (χ^2-value = 24,608.11, p-value < 0.001). This effect can be attributed to higher user engagement on mobile devices (Stewart et al. 2012).

The model-free results show that non-relevant recommendations lead to a higher overall click rate on the focal item. This suggests that introducing non-relevant recommendations can enhance the CTR for the focal item.

4.4   Model and Results

We estimate a logit model with user random effects. Our control variables cover mobile device usage, focal item price and similarity to the base product metrics. Model 1 contains whether the focal recommendation is placed on the second or third position. Hence, the baseline for our analysis is that the product in the first position of the recommendation list is the focal recommendation. The second Model 2 adds the local contrast variables for visual, price and category contrast. The third Model 3 includes an interaction effect between treatment and visual contrast. We chose visual contrast over price or category contrast because the product image is the most prominent factor influencing consumer decisions (Lill and Spann 2022). The results for interaction effects between the treatment and price or category contrast and detailed results on the control variables can be found in the Appendix.

Table 3. Estimation Results: Logit Models with User Random Effects

Variable	Model 1	Model 2	Model 3
(Intercept)	-4.574***	-6.134***	-5.840***
	(0.136)	(0.402)	(0.403)
Treatment	0.256***	0.162**	-0.314
	(0.074)	(0.074)	(0.226)
Focal Item on 2nd Position	0.188***	0.178**	0.218***
	(0.072)	(0.072)	(0.072)
Focal Item on 3rd Position	0.168**	0.139*	0.183**
	(0.073)	(0.072)	(0.073)
Visual Contrast		0.671***	0.410**
		(0.138)	(0.175)
Price Contrast		-0.130	-0.107
		(0.160)	(0.161)
Category Contrast		1.169***	1.022**
		(0.407)	(0.408)
Treatment*Visual Contrast			0.601**
			(0.256)
Observations	*26,973*	*26,973*	*26,973*
AIC	*11,050.25*	*11,011.07*	*11,010.75*

*p < 0.10, **p < 0.05, ***p < 0.01
Notes. Logistic regression models with user-specific random effects. Dependent variable: click on focal item. Control variables: mobile, focal item price, similarity metrics to base product.

Table 3 shows that the treatment effect of displaying non-relevant contrasting recommendations affects the click probability significantly, except for Model 3. This suggests that incorporating contrasting recommendations enhances the focal product's user engagement and CTRs. In Model 3, the treatment effect is insignificant, which can be explained by the positive interaction effect of treatment and visual contrast.

In contrast to Collins et al. (2018), our results indicate that the first position in a list of recommendations is not the most beneficial for accepting the focal recommendation. The results also contradict the conclusion by Murphy et al. (2006) arguing that the most-relevant recommendation should be placed at the beginning of a list. Throughout all models, we consistently find that the second and third positions increase the click probability on the focal item. One possible explanation for this finding is the local contrast effect in line with Häubl et al. (2010). According to this theory, consumers disproportionately react to differences in attractiveness between the current product and the one they inspected immediately before it. This overreaction can make the second and third positions appear more appealing than the first, which users might perceive as a system-preferred or default option. Position 2 seems to be even more beneficial for a focal item. However, the difference between both estimates is not significant (z-value = 0.341, p-value = 0.733).

A possible explanation for the higher significance in click probabilities for position two can be explained by the findings of Guo et al. (2023). As discussed, their research suggests that placing the most relevant recommendation (here, the focal item) in the second position facilitates better user comparison and evaluation. This strategic positioning allows users to engage more thoughtfully with recommendations, leading to higher CTRs for the focal product. Therefore, the results support Hypothesis 1.

Turning to Hypothesis 2, we can see that the contrast between the focal item and its contrasting recommendations significantly increases the CTR. In Model 2, visual contrast (p-value < 0.001) and category contrast (p-value = 0.004) are highly significant. This finding indicates that when the focal product differs in visual appearance or category from the other recommendations, users are more likely to click on the item. The distinctiveness created by these contrasts makes the focal item stand out, increasing its attractiveness and click probability.

When adding the interaction term in Model 3 between treatment and visual contrast, the significance of visual contrast (p-value = 0.013) and category contrast (p-value = 0.012) increases. However, both p-values remain low, suggesting that these contrasts could show even higher significance levels with more data. This slight drop in significance may be due to the complexities introduced by the interaction term, but the overall trend still supports the importance of contrast effects in RS.

Therefore, Hypothesis 2 is supported. The significant p-values in both models demonstrate that higher contrast between the focal product and the contrasting recommendations effectively increases user engagement. This finding aligns with the principle that users are more likely to notice and select items that stand out visually or categorically from their surroundings.

Our last Hypothesis 3 predicts the enhancement of contrast effects by introducing non-relevant recommendations. Model 3 shows that the interaction coefficient is positive and significant (p-value = 0.019). We include the interaction with visual contrast rather than category contrast, because visual cues are the most prominent factor when a user interacts with the recommendations. Category contrast is not as distinctive since it is subject to classification by the retailer's marketing experts, and product categories might overlap.

The positive interaction coefficient indicates that the introduction of non-relevant items amplifies the effect of visual contrast on CTRs. This means that when non-relevant items are included in the recommendation list, the influence of visual contrast on the likelihood of a click on the focal item is enhanced. This significant interaction effect suggests that non-relevant recommendations can make visually distinct focal items even more appealing, thereby increasing CTRs. Therefore, Hypothesis 3 is supported.

4.5   Robustness Test

For robustness checks, we also estimate a user-fixed effects (FE) model. Since a FE logit model can only account for users with at least one click on the focal item (and recommendation views without a click), the number of observations drops to 18,866.

Table 4. Estimation Results: Logit Models with User-Fixed Effects

Variable	Model 1	Model 2
Focal Item on 2nd Position	0.275*** (0.094)	0.276*** (0.095)
Focal Item on 3rd Position	0.185* (0.095)	0.182* (0.096)
Visual Contrast		0.389** (0.198)
Price Contrast		-0.428* (0.242)
Category Contrast		1.007 (0.619)
Observations	*18,866*	*18,866*
AIC	*85,571.81*	*85,565.31*

*p < 0.10, **p < 0.05, ***p < 0.01
Notes. Logistic regression models with user-specific fixed effects. Dependent variable: click on focal item. Control variables: focal item price, similarity metrics to base product.

Table 4 shows that the FE model yields similar position effect results, indicating higher significance for the second position. For the position effect derived from the third position, we obtain a lower significance level. For contrast effects, we only find the positive influence of visual contrast. Category contrast (p-value = 0.104) does not significantly increase the focal item click probability. However, this might be due to the fact that we only account for approximately 70% of the data. Consequently, this could be attributed to the reduced number of observations used to estimate the fixed effects models.

Therefore, a conservative estimate is that the second position in a list of recommendations supports a focal item's CTR. This "middle" position might be more supportive of creating a contrast effect. A possible explanation is that the focal item is surrounded by contrasting recommendations that enhance the comparability. Adding contrast through visually different items than the focal item further helps to increase the likelihood of clicking. Both effects can be explained by the concepts introduced by Häubl et al. (2010) and Guo et al. (2023).

5   Discussion

In our field experiment, we demonstrated that item position and contrast among recommendations influence the acceptance of other recommendations. Our analysis contributed to understanding which attributes significantly affect acceptance rates within a list of recommendations while controlling for the environment in which the recommendations are presented. Hence, our analysis suggests that the contextual environment and the specific attributes of individual recommendations play critical roles in shaping user engagement and acceptance, highlighting the importance of considering these factors when designing RSs and analyzing consumer behavior in RSs.

5.1   Theoretical Implications

Building on this result, our findings provide theoretical implications for the broader understanding of RSs. Specifically, they suggest that the interaction between the contextual environment and individual recommendation attributes may lead to complex behaviors in user acceptance patterns. This underscores the need for more nuanced models for environmental and attribute-based factors. Such models could improve predictive accuracy and enhance the effectiveness of recommendation systems by aligning them more closely with the multifaceted nature of human decision-making processes. Consequently, this research encourages a deeper exploration into the dynamic interplay between context and content in RS, which could pave the way for more sophisticated and user-centric recommendation strategies.

Furthermore, a substantial body of research exists on the effectiveness of RS diversity (Castells et al. 2021). Generally, the literature agrees that higher RS diversity increases user satisfaction by breaking the monotony in recommendations (Zhang and Hurley 2008). Our findings contribute to this understanding by showing that contrasting recommendations, which can be seen as diverse recommendations, increase acceptance rates for a specific recommendation. We argue that diverse recommendations drive increased satisfaction with a focal item, as the variety and contrast make the focal product more appealing by comparison. Hence, diversity indirectly affects user satisfaction by enhancing the attractiveness of the focal recommendations through contrast effects. This reinforces the importance of incorporating diversity into recommendation strategies to improve user engagement and satisfaction and opens a new opportunity for how RS diversity indirectly affects user satisfaction.

5.2   Managerial Implications

Our study highlights that contrasting recommendations significantly influence the CTR of individual recommendations. Hence, we conclude that recommendations are highly affected by the contrasting items. Additionally, the position of a focal (most relevant) recommendation also impacts CTRs. Since user feedback can be directly fed into the RS as implicit feedback (Jannach et al. 2018), the accompanying list of products may bias the resulting recommendations. E-commerce retailers and RS developers should be aware of the effects of position and surrounding recommendations on the user feedback data they use to generate recommendations.

On the other hand, our insights can be leveraged to develop RS that achieve higher CTRs for specific highlighted products. We have seen that contrast within recommendations can boost the CTR of particular recommendations. While this may hurt the overall CTR, it can be strategically used to support and highlight specific products.

However, regulators should be aware that digital platforms could leverage position and contrast effects in RSs to increase the choice of their private label products. By strategically placing their items in positions that benefit from contrast effects, platforms could bias user decisions, leading to a disproportionate selection of platform products over those of third-party sellers. This practice may not align with the principles of fairness and transparency outlined in the Digital Services Act[4], which emphasizes the need for non-discriminatory treatment of content and equal opportunity for all sellers. Regulatory oversight is crucial to ensure RSs are designed and implemented to uphold these standards, preventing platforms from influencing consumer choices unfairly.

---

[4] https://eur-lex.europa.eu/legal-content/EN/TXT/?uri=CELEX%3A32022R2065

5.3   Limitations and Future Research

Our study has several limitations that need to be acknowledged. Firstly, we focused primarily on apparel products. Future research should explore a broader range of product categories to determine if the observed effects hold across various contexts.

Moreover, our study addressed position bias, explaining it as a cognitive bias affecting user evaluation of items. We differentiated this from (bounded) rational heuristics, such as those described by Lerman and Hogg (2014), who attribute the appeal of high-ranked items to reduced search costs. However, our study design included only three items, where search costs among the first, second, or third positions may not differ significantly. Future studies should investigate the optimal number of "preceding" contrasting recommendations, especially in scenarios with longer, scrollable lists, where search costs are likely to vary more substantially.

Additionally, a lab experiment could provide more controlled insights into user behavior and the specific impact of position and contrast effects. A lab setting would allow for manipulating more variables and a more precise measurement of user interactions, helping to isolate the cognitive mechanisms at play. This approach would also remove other confounding effects from the e-commerce platform, offering a clearer view of the factors influencing user behavior. Hence, the underlying mechanisms that drive observed consumer behavior, including search costs and their influence on user interactions with recommendations, could be more thoroughly examined. Understanding these mechanisms could help refine recommendation strategies and enhance their effectiveness across user contexts and product categories.

Appendix

The appendix provides additional estimation results. Table A1 presents results from the random effects model similar to the models from Table 3, exploring the impact of control variables and other interactions between treatment and contrast effects. These supplementary analyses provide additional insights into user behavior within RSs, enhancing the understanding of how contextual effects shape user decision-making.

Table A1 shows that focal item prices consistently increase the click likelihood for the focal item. Higher product prices can increase click rates as they often signal higher quality to consumers, attracting more attention and clicks (Sharma and Garg 2016). Consumers associate higher prices with better quality and prestige, making them more inclined to click on high-priced items to explore their features and benefits. Additionally, the higher price points can create a sense of exclusivity and urgency, prompting consumers to investigate further before potentially making a purchase. In line with Lill and Spann (2022), the results indicate that similarity across the base product and its recommendations is an important driver for recommendation acceptance. Higher visual and category similarity values significantly increase the probability of a click on the focal recommendation. On the other hand, when turning to contrast effects among recommendations, the model shows that visual and category contrast increases the acceptance of the most relevant recommendation.

The results also indicate that contrast effects are lower than the assimilation effects arising from the similarity between the focal product and its recommendations. Specifically, categorical similarity to the base product is essential for consumer acceptance. This reflects the importance of aligning product recommendations with consumer preferences and expectations. Content-based filtering (CBF) algorithms (Ricci et al. 2022) in RS leverage this similarity to enhance the relevance and acceptance of recommended products. This approach ensures that recommendations are tailored to individual user preferences, increasing engagement and satisfaction. Consequently, the effectiveness of RS is significantly improved by focusing on products with higher categorical similarity.

Table A1. Estimation Results: Logit Models with User Random Effects, including control variables and other interaction effects

Variable	Model 1	Model 2	Model 3	Model 4	Model 5
(Intercept)	-4.574*** (0.136)	-6.134*** (0.402)	-5.840*** (0.403)	-6.151*** (0.405)	- 6.044*** (0.427)
Treatment	0.256*** (0.074)	0.162** (0.074)	-0.314 (0.226)	0.721*** (0.245)	-0.180 (0.832)
Mobile	0.008 (0.070)	-0.015 (0.069)	-0.013 (0.069)	-0.012 (0.069)	-0.002 (0.070)
Focal Item Price	0.015*** (0.002)	0.014*** (0.002)	0.014*** (0.002)	0.013*** (0.002)	0.014*** (0.002)
Base Item Visual Similarity	0.672*** (0.143)	0.987*** (0.157)	0.983*** (0.157)	0.981*** (0.157)	1.062*** (0.158)
Base Item Price Similarity	0.017 (0.166)	-0.054 (0.171)	-0.024 (0.171)	0.025 (0.171)	-0.033 (0.172)
Base Item Category Similarity	2.588*** (0.296)	3.368*** (0.378)	3.217*** (0.379)	3.122*** (0.378)	3.227*** (0.382)
Focal Item on 2nd Position	0.188*** (0.072)	0.178** (0.072)	0.218*** (0.072)	0.181** (0.072)	0.188*** (0.072)
Focal Item on 3rd Position	0.168** (0.073)	0.139* (0.072)	0.183** (0.073)	0.149** (0.072)	0.171** (0.073)
Focal Item Visual Contrast		0.671*** (0.138)	0.410** (0.175)	0.702*** (0.138)	0.732*** (0.139)
Focal Item Price Contrast		-0.130 (0.160)	-0.107 (0.161)	0.228 (0.207)	-0.117 (0.161)
Focal Item Category Contrast		1.169*** (0.407)	1.022** (0.408)	0.869** (0.415)	0.928** (0.437)
Treatment*Focal Item Visual Contrast			0.601** (0.256)		
Treatment*Price Contrast				-0.681** (0.288)	
Treatment*Category Contrast					0.375 (0.859)
Observations	26,973	26,973	26,973	26,973	26,973
AIC	11,050.25	11,011.07	11,010.75	11,007.78	11,012.29

*p < 0.10, **p < 0.05, ***p < 0.01

Notes. Logistic regression models with user-specific random effects. Dependent variable: click on focal item. Control variables: mobile, focal item price, similarity metrics to base product.

References

Aivazoglou M, Roussos AO, Margaris D, Vassilakis C, Ioannidis S, Polakis J, Spiliotopoulos D (2020) A fine-grained social network recommender system. *Social Network Analysis and Mining* 10:1-18.

Bless H, Schwarz N (2010) Mental construal and the emergence of assimilation and contrast effects: The inclusion/exclusion model. *Advances in Experimental Social Psychology*, vol. 42 (Elsevier), 319-373.

Castells P, Hurley N, Vargas S (2021) Novelty and diversity in recommender systems. *Recommender Systems Handbook* (Springer), 603-646.

Collins A, Tkaczyk D, Aizawa A, Beel J (2018) Position bias in recommender systems for digital libraries. *International Conference on Information* (Springer), 335-344.

Felfernig A, Friedrich G, Gula B, Hitz M, Kruggel T, Leitner G, Melcher R, Riepan D, Strauss S, Teppan E (2007) Persuasive recommendation: serial position effects in knowledge-based recommender systems. *Persuasive Technology: Second International Conference on Persuasive Technology, PERSUASIVE 2007, Palo Alto, CA, USA, April 26-27, 2007, Revised Selected Papers 2* (Springer), 283-294.

Gai PJ, Klesse A-K (2019) Making recommendations more effective through framings: Impacts of user-versus item-based framings on recommendation click-throughs. *Journal of Marketing* 83(6):61-75.

Gomez-Uribe CA, Hunt N (2015) The netflix recommender system: Algorithms, business value, and innovation. *ACM Transactions on Management Information Systems (TMIS)* 6(4):1-19.

Granka LA, Joachims T, Gay G (2004) Eye-tracking analysis of user behavior in WWW search. *Proceedings of the 27th annual international ACM SIGIR conference on Research and development in information retrieval*, 478-479.

Guo X, Wang L, Zhang M, Chen G (2023) First things first? Order effects in online product recommender systems. *ACM Transactions on Computer-Human Interaction* 30(1):1-35.

Häubl G, Trifts V (2000) Consumer decision making in online shopping environments: The effects of interactive decision aids. *Marketing Science* 19(1):4-21.

Häubl G, Dellaert BGC, Donkers B (2010) Tunnel Vision: Local Behavioral Influences on Consumer Decisions in Product Search. *Marketing Science* 29(3):438-455.

Jannach D, Lerche L, Zanker M (2018) Recommending based on implicit feedback. *Social Information Access* (Springer), 510-569.

Kenrick DT, Gutierres SE (1980) Contrast effects and judgments of physical attractiveness: When beauty becomes a social problem. *Journal of Personality and Social Psychology* 38(1):131.

Krauth K, Wang Y, Jordan MI (2022) Breaking feedback loops in recommender systems with causal inference. *arXiv preprint arXiv:2207.01616*.

Lerman K, Hogg T (2014) Leveraging position bias to improve peer recommendation. *PloS one* 9(6):e98914.

Li X, Grahl J, Hinz O (2022) How Do Recommender Systems Lead to Consumer Purchases? A Causal Mediation Analysis of a Field Experiment. *Information Systems Research* 33(2):620-637.

Lill M, Spann M (2022) Influence of Assimilation Effects on Recommender Systems. *Proceedings of the 43rd International Conference on Information Systems*.

Linden G, Smith B, York J (2003) Amazon.com recommendations: Item-to-item collaborative filtering. *IEEE Internet computing* 7(1):76-80.

Murphy J, Hofacker C, Mizerski R (2006) Primacy and recency effects on clicking behavior. *Journal of computer-mediated communication* 11(2):522-535.

Piramuthu S, Kapoor G, Zhou W, Mauw S (2012) Input online review data and related bias in recommender systems. *Decision Support Systems* 53(3):418-424.

Rafai I, Babutsidze Z, Delahaye T, Hanaki N, Acuna-Agost R (2022) No evidence of attraction effect among recommended options: A large-scale field experiment on an online flight aggregator. *Decision Support Systems* 153(113672):1-11.

Ricci F, Rokach L, Shapira B (2022) *Recommender Systems Handbook* (Springer, Boston, MA, USA).

Schedl M, Knees P, McFee B, Bogdanov D (2021) Music recommendation systems: Techniques, use cases, and challenges. *Recommender Systems Handbook*, vol. 3 (Springer), 927-971.

Schmalenbach K, Gengler E, Laumer S (2022) Promoting Diverse News Consumption Through User Control Mechanisms. *Proceedings of the 43rd International Conference on Information Systems*.

Sharma K, Garg S (2016) An investigation into consumer search and evaluation behaviour: effect of brand name and price perceptions. *Vision* 20(1):24-36.

Stewart C, Hoggan E, Haverinen L, Salamin H, Jacucci G (2012) An Exploration of Inadvertent Variations in Mobile Pressure Input. *Proceedings of the 14th International Conference on Human-Computer Interaction with Mobile Devices and Services*, 35-38.

Strack F, Schwarz N, Gschneidinger E (1985) Happiness and Reminiscing: The Role of Time Perspective, Affect, and Mode of Thinking. *Journal of Personality and Social Psychology* 49(6):1460.

Teppan EC, Zanker M (2015) Decision Biases in Recommender Systems. *Journal of Internet Commerce* 14(2):255-275.

Ursu RM (2018) The power of rankings: Quantifying the effect of rankings on online consumer search and purchase decisions. *Marketing Science* 37(4):530-552.

Zhang M, Hurley N (2008) Avoiding Monotony: Improving the Diversity of Recommendation Lists. *Proceedings of the 2008 ACM Conference on Recommender Systems*, 123-130.

Zhou M, Zhang J, Adomavicius G (2023) Longitudinal impact of preference biases on recommender systems' performance. *Information Systems Research*.

Article 4:
Product Badges and Consumer Choice on Digital Platforms[1]

Markus Lill   Nastasia Gallitz   Lucas Stich   Martin Spann

Digital platforms can strategically influence consumer behavior by shaping the search environment. While previous research has focused primarily on search rankings and recommendations, the effect of product badges has not been systematically studied. This paper investigates how platform-controlled product badges affect consumers' search behavior and product choices on a digital platform. We analyze Amazon data and conduct a series of field experiments using a custom web browser extension developed to experimentally mask badges during the shopping experience. We find considerable heterogeneity in the prevalence, placement, and co-occurrence of different badge types on Amazon. Our experimental studies show that in a multi-badge environment and controlling for product and search characteristics, masking all badges reduces the likelihood of click and add-to-cart for products that received the platform endorsement badge (Amazon's Choice), while increasing these likelihoods for products that received the popularity badge (Best Seller). In single-badge environments, the Best Seller badge significantly increases the likelihood of click and add-to-cart, while the Amazon's Choice badge has no significant effect when controlling for product and search characteristics. This research adds to our understanding of how platform-controlled badges affect consumer behavior and provides insights for consumers, regulators, and sellers in digital marketplaces.

Keywords: Digital platforms, recommender systems, product badges, consumer search & choice

---

[1] This article is based on the following paper: Lill, M., Gallitz, N., Stich, L., and Spann, M. (2024). Product Badges and Consumer Choice on Digital Platforms. *Working Paper, LMU Munich.*

1   Introduction

Through design elements such as recommendations or search result rankings, digital platforms play a significant role in shaping consumer choices (Chen and Tsai 2023, Dinerstein et al. 2018, Farronato et al. 2023). As a result, regulators are increasingly focusing their scrutiny on large digital platforms, such as Google, Facebook, and Amazon (Rietveld and Schilling 2021). The subsequent introduction of new legislation, such as the Digital Services Act (DSA),[2] reflects growing concerns about biases in platform design elements.

Following recent allegations of market power abuse,[3] a nascent stream of literature has begun to examine the design and regulation of digital platforms (Chen and Tsai 2023, Dinerstein et al. 2018, Rietveld and Schilling 2021). A significant portion of this research examines the effects of digital platforms' vertical integration on sellers and consumers, and the consequences of self-preferencing, often from a welfare perspective (Anderson and Bedre-Defolie 2021, Etro 2023, Hagiu et al. 2022, Lee and Musolff 2023, Long and Amaldoss 2024). However, relatively few studies have examined the specific design tools that digital platforms use to influence consumer behavior (Honka et al. 2024). Among these tools, product recommendations (Calvano et al. 2023) and search rankings (Kim et al. 2010, Lam 2023, Ursu 2018) have received the most academic attention (see Appendix A for an overview of the literature on the growing field of platform design and regulation).

While much research and regulatory interest has focused on search rankings, the impact of another crucial platform-provided design element — product badges — on consumer choice has not been systematically studied. Product badges can signal value to consumers, reduce quality uncertainty, and positively influence sales (Cheng et al. 2020, Hui et al. 2016). Additionally, recommendation signage in

---

[2] https://ec.europa.eu/commission/presscorner/detail/en/QANDA_20_2348
[3] For example, https://www.ftc.gov/news-events/news/press-releases/2023/09/ftc-sues-amazon-illegally-maintaining-monopoly-power.

general can affect consumer choice by influencing decision difficulty and the formation of choice sets (Broniarczyk and Griffin 2014, Ghiassaleh et al. 2020, Goodman et al. 2013). However, research specifically on digital platforms' use of badges is comparatively sparse. Existing studies primarily utilize experimental laboratory settings or descriptive observational field data (Cheng et al. 2020, Ghiassaleh et al. 2020, Goodman et al. 2013, Hui et al. 2016).

In this paper, we aim to examine how digital platforms use product badges in their search environments and how these badges affect consumers' search and choice behavior. Specifically, we focus on two product badges that are controlled and assigned by a digital platform: a platform endorsement badge and a seller popularity badge.

In doing so, we make three contributions. First, we examine how a major digital platform, Amazon, employs product badges across a wide range of product categories. By analyzing over 230,000 observations of over 90,000 unique products based on 1,000 search terms over a 50-day period, we explore patterns of badge prevalence, placement, and co-occurrence across various badge types. Our findings reveal considerable heterogeneity in how different badges are assigned and displayed. While advertising- and price-related badges are relatively common, platform endorsement and popularity badges are less common, with only 1.32% and 3.15% of products, respectively, displaying these badges at least once during the observation period. In contrast to all other badge types, we observe that the platform endorsement badge tends to cluster prominently in the top search ranks. Furthermore, while products with a platform endorsement or a popularity badge tend to be higher ranked, less expensive, and better rated on average, we find significant differences across sellers. Specifically, products sold by Amazon exhibit an average price markup of 23.66% compared to badge-assigned products from third-party sellers. Finally, we uncover interesting patterns in the co-occurrence of badges. In particular, platform endorsement and popularity badges are used mutually exclusive, and both types of badges are disproportionately often associated with list prices.[4] Taken together, these findings suggest that there is significant competition for badges on Amazon.

Second, to our knowledge, this paper is among the first to examine how the presence of multiple versus single badges influences consumer choice. Through three field experiments, we find divergent effects of platform endorsement and popularity badges in multi-badge versus single-badge search environments. In particular, our data reveal more complex interactions in multi-badge environments. When both the platform endorsement ("Amazon's Choice") and the popularity badge ("Best Seller") are visible, consumers show a preference for products endorsed by the platform over those highlighted for their popularity (with a 15% click rate for Amazon's Choice compared to a 9% click rate for Best Seller products, and a 14% add-to-cart rate for Amazon's Choice compared to a 7% add-to-cart rate for Best Seller products). In contrast, masking all badges significantly decreases the click and add-to-cart probabilities for Amazon's Choice products (with a 5% click rate and a 4% add-to-cart rate) but increases these probabilities for Best Seller products (with a 12% click rate and 12% add-to-cart rate). These effects persist qualitatively when controlling for product and search characteristics.

However, in environments where only the platform endorsement badge is present, and controlling for product and search characteristics, its influence is less pronounced, failing to significantly influence consumers' choices compared to non-endorsed items. In contrast, in search environments containing only a single popularity badge, and controlling for product and search characteristics, products endorsed for popularity are chosen more frequently than non-endorsed products.

Finally, we developed and evaluated the Product Navigator, a Google Chrome web browser extension. This new tool allows researchers to selectively mask certain platform design elements, such as product badges, to study their impact on

---

[4] For a more detailed account of the implications of list prices, refer to Park et al. (2023).

consumer behavior in real online marketplaces. In doing so, we contribute to the growing body of literature that uses proprietary software to collect consumer clickstream data (e.g., Allcott et al. 2022, Farronato et al. 2024).

2 Product Badges as Platform Design Tools

For the purposes of our research, we classify the badges used by digital platforms into six distinct types: platform endorsement badges, popularity badges, seller-related badges, advertising-related badges, price-related badges, and availability-related badges. Although our empirical analysis is based on Amazon data, these broad types of badges are applicable to other platforms as well. Table 1 provides a classification of badge types along with examples of corresponding Amazon badges.

Table 1. Product Badges Classification

Badge Type	Description	Amazon Examples	Badge Allocation Initiated by
Platform endorsement	Indicates products or sellers that are endorsed, i.e., recommended by the platform itself	Amazon's Choice	Platform
Popularity	Indicates products popular with consumers (in this case: most sold)	Best Seller	Platform
Seller-related	Information about the seller	Climate Pledge Friendly, Small Business	Seller
Advertising-related	Indicates presence of a sponsored advertisement	Sponsored	Seller
Price-related	Any information related to price promotions	Vouchers, Coupons, Limited Time Deal, Lowest Price	Seller
Availability-related	Any information related to product availability and delivery	Prime	Seller

Platform Endorsement Badges

Platform endorsement badges refer to the practice adopted by platforms to prominently highlight and recommend certain products or sellers to consumers (Elfenbein et al. 2015, Hui et al. 2016, Rietveld et al. 2021). However, they are conceptually distinct from related tools, such as advertising, because platforms selectively endorse only a subset of items without allowing sellers to self-select into or purchase a platform endorsement badge (Bairathi et al. 2022). While product sales may play some role in the endorsement badge assignment, platforms do not endorse only top-selling products, and may pursue other strategic goals through this tool (Hukal et al. 2020, Rietveld et al. 2019).

Platform endorsement can facilitate consumer choice by reducing choice overload (Bairathi et al. 2022, Iyengar and Lepper 2000). In addition, platform endorsement can serve as a quality signal (Dewan et al. 2023). As such, it can significantly increase the demand for a good or service (Aguiar and Waldfogel 2018), making it a coveted badge for sellers.[5] An example of this is the "Amazon's Choice" badge, which "highlights highly rated, well-priced products available to ship immediately".[6] Other examples are eBay's "Top-Rated Seller", Taobao.com's "Gold Medal Seller", or AirBnB's "Superhost".

Popularity Badges

While platforms assign endorsement badges based on criteria that may vary in transparency, popularity badges, often labeled as "Best Seller" or "Top-Selling", are primarily awarded based on product demand observed by the platform. In general, popularity information can create a positive feedback loop that reinforces high demand for a good or service (Cai et al. 2009, Carare 2012, Salganik et al. 2006). However, the effectiveness of popularity information in influencing consumer choice can be affected by certain contextual factors (Tucker and Zhang 2011). For example, products labeled as "Best Seller" may increase decision difficulty by inducing decision uncertainty, especially in the presence of

---

[5] Several online practitioner's guides describe the importance of and strategies for obtaining platform endorsement badges. See https://www.edesk.com/blog/amazon-choice-badge/ for an Amazon-specific example.
[6] This description of the Amazon's Choice badge is displayed when hovering over the badge on a product detail page. More information can be found on
https://www.amazon.com/b?ie=UTF8&node=21449952011.

incongruence between consumer preferences and the endorsement (Ghiassaleh et al. 2020, Goodman et al. 2013).

Seller-Related Badges

We classify seller-related badges as any form of seller information or seller certification that is not a platform endorsement. Third-party sellers on Amazon can earn certifications such as the "Climate Pledge Friendly" or the "Small Business" badge. Although the impact of these certifications on consumer choice remains yet to be investigated, eco-labels or information about firm size may positively shape consumer attitudes and expectations toward sellers (Atkinson and Rosenthal 2014, Yang and Aggarwal 2019). Importantly, in the Amazon context, these badges are not initiated by the platform; instead, sellers initiate the certification process.

Advertising-Related Badges

Advertising-related badges refer to sponsored or paid search results, where advertisers pay to have their search results displayed prominently alongside organic search results (Blake et al. 2015, Ghose and Yang 2009). Although associated with higher click-through rates and revenues, sponsored search ads do not always enter consumers' consideration and choice sets. Factors such as competition (Yang et al. 2014) or seller attributes (Dai et al. 2023, Jerath et al. 2011) can significantly influence the impact of sponsored search ads on consumer behavior. On Amazon, sponsored search ads are indicated by a "Sponsored" badge, which often coincides with higher positions on the search page or prominent display in product carousels. While this badge has the potential to activate consumers' persuasive knowledge (Friestad and Wright 1994), it is more likely that any effects on consumer behavior are due to the associated position of the sponsored product rather than the badge itself (Long and Amaldoss 2024). Since sellers decide whether to advertise their products, it is ultimately the seller who initiates the assignment of the badge.

Price-Related Badges

Price-related badges provide information about price promotions, which typically have a positive effect on product demand in the short run (Blattberg et al. 1995). On Amazon, we identify several types of coupons — those offering a percentage discount and those offering an absolute monetary discount — and the Limited Time Deal badge as important forms of price-related badges. The latter implies a time constraint, which can increase the effectiveness of a promotion (Eisenbeiss et al. 2015, Inman et al. 1997). Since sellers manage such promotions independently, they are the ones who initiate the allocation of badges.

Availability-Related Badges

Availability-related badges refer to a product's availability, especially low stock levels, and delivery terms of a product. Disclosing low stock levels can signal scarcity, which can increase sales of the focal product and induce spillover effects for less preferred products (Cui et al. 2019, Cui and Shin 2018). Similarly, delivery times are essential, especially in online retailing (Brynjolfsson et al. 2009, Kumar et al. 1997), with long delivery times or waiting times that deviate from the originally communicated delivery showing detrimental effects on sales and repurchase behavior (Cui et al. 2020, Harter et al. 2024). In addition to inventory and delivery information, Amazon uses a "Prime" badge to indicate items eligible for one-day Prime delivery. By increasing consumer welfare, consumers view Prime delivery positively (Iyengar et al. 2023). It is important to note, however, that the display of the Prime badge varies depending on whether consumers are logged into their Amazon accounts and whether they subscribe to Amazon Prime.[7]

---

[7] https://www.amazon.com/amazonprime/?sr=53-1.

3   Prevalence and Use of Product Badges on Amazon

3.1   Method

To investigate the prevalence and usage of badges, we collected data on Amazon Germany using a custom web-scraping algorithm. Over a period of 50 days, we analyzed search results and product detail pages (PDPs) for 1,000 search terms. We compiled a comprehensive list of search terms by identifying 10 different categories on Amazon. For each category, we derived 100 search terms using ChatGPT ensuring that they reflected the breadth of products within each category. Following this generation process, we manually reviewed the list to eliminate duplicates and verify the alignment of search terms with their respective categories. Since certain search terms may fit into multiple categories, we resampled overlapping search terms to ensure the quality and relevance of our dataset (see Table B1 in the Appendix B).

Our algorithm simulated consumer searches by randomly selecting terms from our list. Each term triggered the opening of an automated browser window that navigated to the corresponding search results page on Amazon. To maintain anonymity, the algorithm rotated user agents with each request, and all cookies were cleared when the web page was closed. For each search term, the algorithm extracted data from the first search results page, including the search layout design (list or grid) and product-specific attributes such as average ratings, prices, and badges per product. This approach is consistent with established methods in the field (Gutierrez 2021, Lam 2023, Peng and Liang 2023).

We downloaded the product images displayed on the search results page, associated each with its Amazon Serial Identification Number (ASIN) to ensure uniqueness, and linked the images to their respective product attributes. Our algorithm also extended the scraping to the PDPs for each search result, extracting granular product data such as seller information, fulfillment details, Best Seller rank, rating distribution, and top comments. To avoid overloading Amazon's servers and to adhere to good research practices, we included a 15-second delay between each page scrape.

3.2 Results

Our data collection efforts yielded a dataset comprising of 231,547 search result entries and identified 92,228 unique products, revealing the use of 10 different product badges by Amazon (see Table 1 "Amazon examples"). We begin by examining the frequency and patterns of badge assignments among unique products (i.e., individual search results) and search terms on Amazon Germany. Figure 1 illustrates the distribution of badges, providing a comparative view between individual products and overarching search terms.

Figure 1. Badge Occurrence Across Products and Search Terms

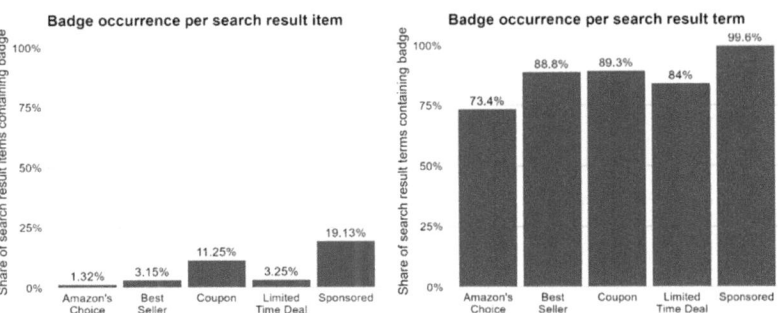

The data reveal a nuanced approach to the allocation of platform endorsement ("Amazon's Choice") and popularity ("Best Seller") badges. Only 1.32% of products receive the Amazon's Choice platform endorsement badge, and 3.15% receive the Best Seller popularity badge. This selective distribution also extends to the search term level: over a 50-day period, only 73.4% of search terms contain at least one Amazon's Choice product. This relative scarcity, compared to other badge types, underscores the competitive nature of the Amazon's Choice and Best Seller badges. Table B2 in the Appendix B compares the average prices, average ratings, and average ranks of Amazon's Choice and Best Seller products with those that do not bear either badge, along with the number of products in each category. In addition, we distinguish between products sold by Amazon and those sold by third-party sellers.

Our results show that products with either Amazon's Choice or Best Seller badges are consistently less expensive than unbadged products within the same categories. In addition, these badged products have higher average ratings and better ranks. Notably, products sold by Amazon have an average price premium of 8.81€ (23.66%) compared to products sold by third-party sellers. This markup is even more pronounced for Best Seller products, with Amazon-sold bestsellers averaging about 15.82€ (44.13%) more than their third-party-sold counterparts.

In addition, we find that products sold by Amazon are disproportionately more often represented among both types of badges. While 38.5% of Amazon's Choice products are sold by Amazon, only 21.5% of non-Amazon's Choice products in the same category are sold by Amazon, and only 23.5% of all products are sold by Amazon. Although these differences are less pronounced for Best Seller products, Amazon still sells 33.1% of bestsellers compared to 22.9% of non-Best Seller products in the same categories.

Given the potential influence of badges on consumer behavior, we further analyze search result rankings. Figure 2 shows box plots of rankings for six types of badges found on Amazon. Notably, the Amazon's Choice badge (leftmost plot) is particularly associated with top search ranks. While price-related badges are fairly evenly distributed across the entire search page, products labeled as Amazon's Choice, Best Seller, or Sponsored are more likely to be found in the top half of search pages. Despite being the second rarest badge type, the Best Seller badge is relatively evenly distributed across the top half of search results. In contrast, the Amazon's Choice badge is heavily clustered in the top ranks, even more so than sponsored products, which represent paid search results. Figures B1 and B2 in the Appendix show search rank distributions for the same badges by display format (search grid vs. search list) and reveal identical distribution patterns across badge types.

Figure 2. Search Rank Distribution by Badge Type (Per Search Term, All Formats)

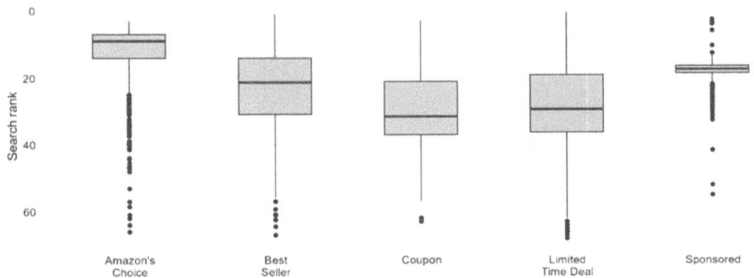

Conceivably, there are differences in how Amazon employs the Amazon's Choice and Best Seller badges, even though these badges have a similarly competitive nature. Both badges are placed in the upper left corner of a product image in search results, making their use mutually exclusive. In fact, the two badges never co-occur in our dataset, suggesting that Amazon strictly separates popularity from platform endorsement badges.

In addition, we observe patterns of co-occurrence with other product information and badges: First, the Amazon's Choice and Best Seller badges occur disproportionately more common with list (and strike) prices compared to the overall sample. Specifically, 33.61% of all products have a list price, while 50.67% of Amazon's Choice products and 56.06% of Best Seller products have a list price. Second, price promotions, such as coupons, are far less likely to co-occur with either the Amazon's Choice (9.17%) or Best Seller (10.16%) badges. Similarly, only 0.08% of Amazon's Choice and 0.3% of Best Seller products co-occur with Limited Time Deals. Finally, only 10.34% of Amazon's Choice products co-occur with a Sponsored badge, which is disproportionately less often than in the overall sample (19.13%). Conversely, Best Seller products co-occur with Sponsored badges slightly more often (17.58%).

3.3   Discussion

Our findings reveal a selective allocation of Amazon's Choice and Best Seller badges on Amazon. The data show a marked rarity in the assignment of these badges, with only 1.32% of products receiving Amazon's Choice and 3.15% receiving the Best Seller badge.

This selectivity, combined with the fact that Amazon's Choice and Best Seller products' are associated with lower prices and higher ratings, suggests a competitive nature associated with these badge types. In particular, products sold by Amazon have a substantial price premium and appear to receive these badges disproportionately more often than products sold by third-party sellers.

4   Effects of Product Badges on Consumer Behavior: Experimental Studies

Following the findings on the variety and different patterns of badge allocation in Section 3, we next examine the impact of these badges on consumer behavior. Our subsequent analyses examine how badges, both in combination and in isolation, influence consumer search and choice. We conduct three experimental studies using a custom-developed browser extension.

4.1   Methodology

4.1.1   Browser Extension

To study the impact of platform badges on consumer behavior in the field, we developed a Chrome extension called "Product Navigator". This tool allows researchers to dynamically modify the appearance of Amazon search results pages while simultaneously collecting user interaction data. The extension can also randomly assign participants to different experimental groups, allowing the presentation of search results to be tailored to the objectives of each specific study. Figure 3 illustrates the functionality of the extension by contrasting an unmodified search results page (left panel) with a version in which item information other than product description, price, and consumer rating is masked by the extension (right panel). The extension allows researchers to choose which information to mask. In the experimental studies, certain badges remain visible in one group while being masked in the other. In addition, the extension disables filtering, sorting, and pagination features on Amazon's search results pages to facilitate the analysis of user search behavior.

Figure 3. Example of Search Result Modifications Using the Chrome Extension "Product Navigator" (Left: Unmodified Results, Right: Masked Item Information)

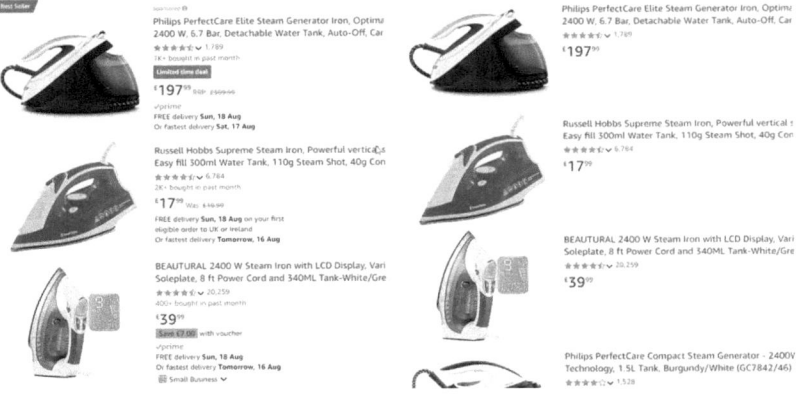

Participants in the experiments receive a personal identifier to ensure accurate assignments of participants to their experimental groups, track their behavior, and prevent crossover effects. The tracking methodology is highly granular, capturing page views and individual interactions with each search result. This includes verifying that a product from the Amazon search result page is fully visible in the participant's viewport, ensuring that the participant can view all available product information. Additionally, we differentiate between direct product clicks and those that open in a new tab, providing insight into the participant's level of engagement with the platform. All information displayed is collected consistently and in real time.

Additionally, the tool can distinguish whether participants are actively viewing a page or opening pages in a background tab. In the latter case, the tool triggers an event that captures the moment a participant navigates back to the Amazon web page. This distinction allows us to infer the level of attention participants are paying to the content presented, further enriching our understanding of consumer behavior on the platform.

It is important to note that our data collection respects the privacy of all participants. All personal information collected through cookies is deleted once a participant completes a session by adding a product to their shopping cart. Participants are also instructed to uninstall the extension upon completion of the study to ensure the end of data tracking. In all studies, participants gave their consent to the experimental procedure.

4.1.2   Experimental Paradigm

In all three field experiments, we recruited participants through Prolific UK, a widely recognized online platform for participant sourcing.

As part of the study, participants were required to install the Product Navigator extension from the Google Chrome Web Store. After verifying successful installation, participants were randomly assigned to one of two experimental groups. Each group was exposed to different browser-side modifications of the search results pages on Amazon UK. The first group consistently interacted with a streamlined version of the actual Amazon search results page, where the browser extension masked all of the badges specified in Section 2 (see Table 1). The second group viewed modifications of the Amazon search results pages according to the respective experimental settings. Granular details of the exact modifications are given in the subsections below. We masked recommendation carousels and ads for both experimental groups and limited results to the first search page to make the groups as comparable as possible.

Following the group assignment, participants were instructed to browse the Amazon UK search results page for the keyword "toaster" and add the product they were most likely to buy to their shopping cart. We chose toasters as the focal product for our experiments based on the notion that, in the context of low-cost, utilitarian goods, such as toasters, consumer decisions are less likely to be influenced by brand loyalty. We provided a direct link to the specific Amazon search results page to ensure consistency in the browsing experience and reduce individual task completion errors (e.g., searching "toasters" rather than "toaster"). To maintain the integrity of participant tracking and group assignment, the Amazon search results page URL included two custom query parameters to capture the unique Prolific User ID and the group assignment.

When the Amazon search results page was opened, the Product Navigator extension automatically read the custom query parameters embedded in the URL. This allowed the Amazon search results page to be immediately modified according to the predefined group characteristics. Therefore, we ensured that the web page and group modifications were loaded after the group assignment was read from the extension, eliminating any risk of crossover effects that might have resulted from inadvertent exposure to other group configurations.

Participants were given unlimited time to complete the task and were able to browse the search results at their own pace, using standard browser features, such as backward navigation. They could view product details by clicking on the product from the search results list. From the PDP, participants could use either the add-to-cart button or the buy-now button. In both cases, a pop-up notification appeared indicating successful completion of the task. At the end of the experiment, participants were compensated for their time and participation.

We filter out participants who did not follow the experimental instructions, e.g., by searching for products other than the one specified. We also exclude participants for whom we did not record an add-to-cart event, as well as participants for whom we recorded multiple add-to-cart events for different products. In the case of multiple add-to-cart events for the same product, we filter out all events registered after the first add-to-cart event. Finally, we exclude participants with missing data. We did not find any significant relationship between the filtering criteria and the experimental treatments.

4.1.3   Model

As described in Section 4.1.1, the extension captures all participant interactions with the Amazon search results page and PDPs at the event level, identifying unique participants by their Prolific ID and storing the data in a proprietary database. In addition, our dataset contains information on product attributes displayed and removed, including badge details.

To estimate the likelihood of consumers clicking on a product or adding it to their cart, we use logit models and control for various product and search characteristics (see Equation 1).

(1) $y_{ij} = \beta_0 + masked_{ij} + badges_{ij} + masked_{ij} \times badges_{ij} + PRC_{ij} + \epsilon_{ij}$
       with $y_{ij} \in \{click_{ij}, addToCart_{ij}\}$

The dependent variables $click_{ij}$ (and $addToCart_{ij}$) denote binary vectors indicating whether participant i clicked on product j or added it to their cart. The variable $masked_{ij}$ denotes the treatment condition, indicating whether participant i viewed a product j with masked badges. The variable $badges_{ij}$ represents a vector of dummy variables indicating whether participant i viewed a product j labeled with the respective badge. The variable PRC_{ij} denotes a vector of product-related control variables, while ϵ_{ij} represents the error term. To examine the individual badge-specific effect and to disentangle the direct badge effect from product characteristics, we compute interaction effects $masked_{ij} \times badges_{ij}$ between the examined badges and badge visibility.

To account for the nested panel data structure, we cluster standard errors at the participant level. This method accounts for the inherent correlations that arise when multiple observations are derived from the same participant, which may be due to shared characteristics, preferences, behaviors, or other common factors. By clustering standard errors in this way, we aim to improve the reliability and robustness of statistical inference by accounting for intra-cluster correlations (Cameron and Miller 2015).

4.2 Experiment 1: Effects of Multiple Badges on Consumer Search and Choice

4.2.1 Method and Data

To investigate the effects of multi-badge search environments on consumer search behavior and product choice, we conducted a two-group, between-participants field experiment. We recruited $n = 250$ participants from Prolific UK and asked them to install the Product Navigator extension from the Chrome Web Store. Participants were compensated a total of £2.25.

We randomly assigned participants to one of two experimental groups. While all badges remained visible in the "badges visible" group, we hid all badge information in the "badges masked" group.[8] After excluding 14 participants who did not add a

---

[8] The "badges visible" group represented the typical Amazon experience at the time of the experiment, showing badges and additional details like delivery times, view counts, and data on how frequently a particular toaster had been purchased. In contrast, the "badges masked" group hid these visuals from the search results page.

product to their cart, 3 participants who added more than one product to their cart, and 34 participants with incomplete data, we obtained a sample of $n = 212$ participants (M_{age} = 42 years; *Female* = 56%; $M_{duration}$ = 6 min 10 sec).

Table 2 presents descriptive statistics and model-free results that reveal notable differences in search and choice behavior across experimental conditions. Using a series of Mann-Whitney [9] and χ^2-tests, we first find that masking badges significantly increases the average number of views per participant. In addition, we observe differences in click and add-to-cart behavior associated with the Amazon's Choice and Limited Time Deal badges. Specifically, participants tend to click significantly less on Amazon's Choice and Limited Time Deal products when all badges are masked. The same trend is observed for add-to-cart events. Interestingly, while the χ^2-test did not reveal a significant difference, we see a reversal in behavior for Best Seller products: Participants in the "badges masked" condition show a higher propensity to click on and add Best Seller products to their cart compared to participants in the "badges visible" condition.

---

[9] We compute both parametric Welch tests and non-parametric Mann-Whitney tests, but report only the latter due to the non-normality of the data examined. However, Welch tests yield qualitatively equivalent results.

Table 2. Descriptive Statistics and Model Free Results from Experiment 1

	Badges Visible		Badges Masked		Test statistic (p-value)
	$M(\sigma)$	$[min; max]$	$M(\sigma)$	$[min; max]$	
Views	18.66 (12.90)	[0;82]	22.27 (13.70)	[2;70]	$W = 4731$ (0.05)
Click	1.55 (1.33)	[0;9]	1.33 (0.86)	[0;5]	$W = 5914$ (0.38)
Time-to-cart (in sec)	83.26 (77.10)	[10.90;451]	77.19 (63.20)	[13.10;372]	$W = 5647$ (0.47)
Amazon's Choice: Click	0.15	-	0.05	-	$\chi^2 = 5.95$ (0.01)
Amazon's Choice: Add-to-cart	0.14	-	0.04	-	$\chi^2 = 6.55$ (0.01)
Best Seller: Click	0.09	-	0.12	-	$\chi^2 = 0.58$ (0.45)
Best Seller: Add-to-cart	0.07	-	0.12	-	$\chi^2 = 1.06$ (0.30)
Limited time deal: Click	0.11	-	0.00	-	$\chi^2 = 12.25$ (< 0.01)
Limited time deal: Add-to-cart	0.07	-	0.00	-	$\chi^2 = 8.01$ (< 0.01)
Sponsored: Click	0.32	-	0.39	-	$\chi^2 = 1.14$ (0.29)
Sponsored: Add-to-cart	0.27	-	0.37	-	$\chi^2 = 2.32$ (0.13)
Observations	108	108	104	104	212

Notes. We test mean differences in views, clicks, and time-to-cart between experimental conditions using Mann-Whitney tests, and badge-specific differences using Chi-Squared tests.

4.2.2   Model Results

Next, we formally analyze participants' search and selection behavior. When a participant clicks on a product from the search results, they are redirected to the PDP. In addition, we estimate the probability that a participant will add a product to their cart depending on several product and search environment characteristics, namely the products' average rating, number of ratings, search rank, price, and Amazon Prime delivery.

The first two columns of Table 3 present regression results with click as the dependent variable. The effect of badge masking, i.e., making badges invisible, on participants' likelihood to click consistently shows a negative and significant effect in both models. In addition, Amazon's Choice, Best Seller, and Limited Time Deal products each have a significant, positive direct effect on participants' likelihood to click, indicating that participants are more likely to click on products marked with these badges.

To determine whether these direct badge effects are primarily due to product characteristics or are additionally influenced by increased salience due to the display of a visual badge cue, we compute interaction effects between the badges and badge visibility in Model II. Our analysis shows that participants are significantly less likely to click on an Amazon's Choice product ($\beta = -1.217, p < 0.10$) as well as on a Limited Time Deal product ($\beta = -15.288, p < 0.01$) when all badges are masked. Conversely, the positive interaction between masked badges and Best Seller products ($\beta = 1.353, p < 0.05$) suggests a mitigated, if not reversed, effect in this context.

In the last two columns of Table 3, we present the results for the models with add-to-cart as the dependent variable. The negative coefficient in Model III indicates that masking badges decreases the likelihood of items being added to a participant's cart. However, the coefficient becomes insignificant when accounting for the effects of individual badges.

Table 3. Regression Results for Experiment 1

Model:	I	II	III	IV
Dependent variable:	**Click**	**Click**	**Add-to-Cart**	**Add-to-Cart**
Constant	-4.576***	-4.554***	-4.665***	-4.638***
	(0.997)	(1.012)	(1.089)	(1.092)
Badges masked	-0.310***	-0.636*	-0.151**	-0.539
	(0.118)	(0.353)	(0.075)	(0.384)
Average rating	0.056**	0.059**	0.046*	0.050*
	(0.024)	(0.025)	(0.027)	(0.027)
Number of ratings	-2×10^{-4}**	-2×10^{-4}**	-1×10^{-4}	-1×10^{-4}
	(1×10^{-4})	(1×10^{-4})	(1×10^{-4})	(1×10^{-4})
Search rank	-0.040***	-0.042***	-0.030***	-0.031***
	(0.010)	(0.010)	(0.010)	(0.010)
Price	1×10^{-6}***	1×10^{-6}***	1×10^{-6}***	1×10^{-6}***
	(1×10^{-7})	(1×10^{-7})	(1×10^{-7})	(1×10^{-7})
Amazon's Choice product	1.303**	1.822***	0.864	1.464**
	(0.587)	(0.641)	(0.560)	(0.604)
Best Seller product	2.301***	1.732***	2.141***	1.597***
	(0.407)	(0.468)	(0.422)	(0.500)
Limited Time Deal product	0.375	1.137***	-0.013	0.727
	(0.357)	(0.393)	(0.439)	(0.476)
Sponsored product	-0.139	-0.372	-0.111	-0.386
	(0.165)	(0.228)	(0.178)	(0.246)
On sale	0.457***	0.286	0.574***	0.412
	(0.163)	(0.205)	(0.193)	(0.2614)
Amazon Prime delivery	0.286*	0.312	0.133	0.080
	(0.152)	(0.230)	(0.147)	(0.246)
Badges masked × Amazon's Choice product		-1.217*		-1.513**
		(0.661)		(0.723)
Badges masked × Best Seller product		1.353**		1.218*
		(0.576)		(0.625)
Badges masked × Limited Time Deal product		-15.288***		-14.785***
		(0.562)		(0.601)
Badges masked × Sponsored product		0.478		0.513
		(0.310)		(0.340)
Badges masked × On sale		0.371		0.318
		(0.314)		(0.364)
Badges masked × Amazon Prime delivery		0.015		0.158
		(0.309)		(0.307)
Observations	3,391	3,391	3,391	3,391
Log-Likelihood	-877.00	-864.00	-743.00	-731.00
Pseudo R^2	0.039	0.053	0.033	0.048

Notes. Dependent variables: click & add-to-cart. Clustered standard errors (by user ID) in parentheses.
*** $p < 0.01$, ** $p < 0.05$, * $p < 0.1$

Models III and IV show that participants are significantly more likely to add Best Seller products to their carts. While the coefficient for Amazon's Choice products is insignificant in Model III, it has a significant positive effect in Model IV. Limited Time Deal products show no significant effects in Models III and IV.

The significant negative interaction between badge masking and Amazon's Choice products suggests that the absence of platform endorsement significantly decreases the likelihood of these items being added to a participant's cart. The positive interaction between badge masking and Best Seller products, although only marginally significant, suggests a mitigated, if not reversed, negative impact of masked badges on these items. In addition, a significant negative interaction between masked badges and Limited Time Deal products indicates that participants are significantly less likely to add such items to their cart when badges are not visible. This, in turn, suggests that the entry of Limited Time Deal products into participants' choice set may be driven solely by the visual cue signaling urgency.

Finally, we examine the effect of badge presence on participants' time-to-cart, which is the time elapsed between accessing Amazon UK, denoted by the first page-load event registered for a particular participant, and a participant's first add-to-cart event. However, we do not find a significant difference between participants who see badges and those who do not. Detailed results for time-to-cart are reported in Appendix C.

4.2.3   Discussion

Masking badges significantly reduces the overall likelihood that consumers will click on products, suggesting a reduction in consideration set size. Similarly, masking badges significantly reduces the likelihood that Amazon's Choice and Limited Time Deal products' will be clicked or added to consumers' carts. The Best Seller badge shows the opposite pattern: Masking the Best Seller badge increases the likelihood of clicking on the Best Seller product and adding it to the cart.

While a detailed investigation of the mechanism driving these results is beyond the scope of this paper, search costs (Weitzman 1979) appear to be a candidate explanation for the observed patterns. Specifically, we suggest that, similar to rankings (Ursu 2018), badges may reduce search costs.

As for the countervailing effect of the Best Seller badge, two opposing explanations are possible. First, search results that include both a product with an Amazon's Choice badge and a product with the Best Seller badge may increase consumer choice difficulty, since both badges represent a recommendation — based on a platform endorsement in the former case, and based on the popularity among other consumers in the latter case. A subset of consumers may interpret a platform endorsement as being more objective or trustworthy, and thus choose to follow the platform's recommendation. Second, consumers' need for uniqueness may induce reactance to popularity cues such as Best Seller badges (Steinhart et al. 2014, Wu and Lee 2016).

4.3   Experiment 2: Effects of the Amazon's Choice Badge in Isolation

4.3.1   Method and Data

The second experiment aims to isolate the effect of the Amazon's Choice badge on consumers' search behavior and product choice. To this end, we conducted a two-group between-participants field experiment. We recruited $n = 400$ participants[10] from Prolific UK and asked them to install the Product Navigator extension. Participants were compensated with a total of £1.50. In addition, we implemented an incentive alignment mechanism similar to Häubl and Trifts (2000). Specifically, participants were informed that if they successfully completed the study, they would be entered into a lottery in which three randomly selected participants would

---

[10] None of these participants participated in the other experimental studies described in this paper.

win their chosen product as well as a voucher for the difference between £60 and the value of the chosen product.[11]

After confirming that participants had correctly installed the extension, we instructed them to browse the Amazon UK search results page for the keyword "toaster" and add the product that they were most likely to buy to their shopping cart. Participants were randomly assigned to one of two experimental groups. In addition to the elements specified in experiment 1, we masked all badges except for the Amazon's Choice badge in the "Amazon's Choice badge visible" condition and hid all badges for participants in the "Amazon's Choice badge masked" condition. After filtering out 38 participants with incomplete data and 40 participants who did not add a product to their cart, we obtained a sample of $n = 322$ participants ($M_{age} = 38$ years; $Female = 55\%$; $M_{duration} = 6$ min 14 sec).

Table 4 presents descriptive statistics as well as model-free results indicating slight differences in participant behavior between the two experimental groups. A non-parametric Mann-Whitney test[12] indicates no significant differences in the number of clicks between participants who see an Amazon's Choice badge and participants who do not see any badges. However, χ^2-tests indicate marginally significant differences between the experimental groups in the likelihood of clicking on the Amazon's Choice product, i.e., the proportion of participants clicking on the Amazon's Choice product when the badge is visible is higher than the proportion of participants clicking on the Amazon's Choice product when the badge is masked. Differences in the proportion of participants who add an Amazon's Choice product

---

[11] While the instructions for our study stated these terms, the winners were free to choose between the announced lottery prize and a £60 bonus payment via Prolific. This choice was not disclosed to other study participants.

[12] We compute both parametric Welch tests and non-parametric Mann-Whitney tests, but report only the latter due to the non-normality of the data examined. However, Welch tests yield qualitatively equivalent results.

to their cart when the badge is visible vs. when the badge is masked are not significant.

Table 4. Descriptive Statistics and Model Free Results from Experiment 2

	Amazon's Choice Visible		Amazon's Choice Masked		Test statistic (p-value)
	$M (\sigma)$	$[min; max]$	$M (\sigma)$	$[min; max]$	
Views	21.5 (12.70)	[0;81]	21.1 (10.60)	[3;62]	$W = 12760$ (0.40)
Clicks	1.54 (1.11)	[0;8]	1.45 (0.87)	[1;6]	$W = 13181$ (0.37)
Time-to-cart (in sec)	90.80 (78.40)	[11.90;462]	83.70 (59.70)	[14.9;364]	$W = 13012$ (0.48)
Amazon's Choice: Clicks	0.14	-	0.08	-	$\chi^2 = 3.73$ (0.05)
Amazon's Choice: Add-to-carts	0.12	-	0.08	-	$\chi^2 = 1.65$ (0.20)
Observations	162	162	160	160	322

Notes. We test mean differences in views, clicks, and time-to-cart between experimental conditions using Mann-Whitney tests, and badge-specific differences using Chi-Squared tests.

4.3.2   Model and Results

Analogous to experiment 1, we use logit models to estimate the likelihood that a participant will click on a product and add it to their cart, respectively. The first two columns of Table 5 report the regression results for the models with click as the dependent variable.

In Models I-II, masking only the Amazon's Choice badge does not have a statistically significant effect. Furthermore, while the coefficient in Model I is negative, Model II shows a positive, albeit insignificant, coefficient, indicating no clear pattern of influence on click behavior based on badge visibility.

The coefficients for Amazon's Choice products in Models I and II are insignificant, indicating no significant differences in click likelihood between endorsed and non-endorsed products. The interaction between masked Amazon's Choice badge and the Amazon's Choice product is negative, but not statistically significant. In conclusion, in the absence of other badges, the Amazon's Choice badge does not significantly influence participants' click behavior when controlling for other product and search environment characteristics.

We report regression results for the models with add-to-cart as the dependent variable in the last two columns of Table 5. Similar to our results for click behavior, masking only the Amazon's Choice badge does not have a statistically significant effect on a participant's likelihood of adding an item to their cart. Similarly, neither the coefficients denoting an Amazon's Choice product nor the interaction term between badge masking and the Amazon's Choice product show a significant effect on participants' product choices.

Table 5. Regression Results for Experiment 2

Model:	I	II	III	IV
Dependent variable:	**Click**	**Click**	**Add-to-Cart**	**Add-to-Cart**
Constant	-4.462***	-4.489***	-5.960***	-5.982***
	(0.967)	(0.966)	(1.145)	(1.144)
Amazon's Choice masked	-0.042	0.012	-0.013	0.028
	(0.065)	(0.075)	(0.039)	(0.055)
Average rating	0.041*	0.041*	0.069***	0.069***
	(0.023)	(0.023)	(0.027)	(0.027)
Number of ratings	1×10^{-4}***	1×10^{-4}***	1×10^{-4}***	1×10^{-4}***
	(3×10^{-5})	(3×10^{-5})	(3×10^{-5})	(3×10^{-5})
Position	-0.024***	-0.024***	-0.023***	-0.022***
	(0.007)	(0.007)	(0.008)	(0.008)
Price	1×10^{-4}***	1×10^{-4}***	1×10^{-4}***	1×10^{-4}***
	(2×10^{-5})	(2×10^{-5})	(2×10^{-5})	(2×10^{-5})
Amazon's Choice product	-0.313	-0.023	-0.214	-0.008
	(0.265)	(0.311)	(0.279)	(0.335)
Amazon's Choice masked × Amazon's Choice product		-0.676		-0.457
		(0.420)		(0.438)
Observations	5,631	5,631	5,631	5,631
Log-Likelihood	-1,410.00	-1,408.00	-1,184.00	-1,184.00
Pseudo R^2	0.021	0.023	0.025	0.025

Notes. Dependent variables: click & add-to-cart. Clustered standard errors (by user ID) in parentheses.
*** p < 0.01, ** p < 0.05, * p < 0.1

Finally, we examine the effect of badge visibility on participants' time-to-cart. However, a negative effect of masking the Amazon's Choice badge is not significant. We report detailed results on time-to-cart in Appendix C.

4.3.3   Discussion

When examined in isolation, the Amazon's Choice badge does not appear to significantly affect consumer behavior when we control for product and search environment characteristics such as search ranking or product rating. The difference from the findings of experiment 1 may be partially due to the less complex search environment provided in this experiment. To isolate the platform endorsement badge, we masked all other badges in both experimental conditions, which may have reduced the information load and thus the need to rely on a heuristic such as the platform endorsement for decision making (Malhotra 1982).

4.4   Experiment 3: Effects of the Best Seller Badge in Isolation

4.4.1   Method and Data

Experiment 3 examines the Best Seller badge. We employed an experimental design similar to experiment 2. We recruited $n = 400$ participants[13] from Prolific UK and asked them to install the Product Navigator extension. Participants were compensated with a total of £1.50. In line with experiment 2, we implemented an incentive alignment mechanism similar to Häubl and Trifts (2000). Specifically, participants were informed that if they successfully completed the study, they would be entered into a lottery in which three randomly selected participants would

---

[13] None of these participants participated in the other experimental studies described in this paper.

win their chosen product as well as a voucher for the difference between £60 and the value of the chosen product.[14]

After verifying that participants had correctly installed the extension, we asked them to browse the Amazon UK search results page for the keyword "toaster" and add the product that they were most likely to buy to their shopping cart. Participants were randomly assigned to one of two experimental groups. In the "Best Seller badge visible" condition, we masked all badges except the Best Seller badge. In the "Best Seller badge masked" condition, we masked all badges. After filtering out 38 participants who did not add a product to their cart, 2 participants who added multiple products to their cart, 38 participants with incomplete data, and 23 participants who did not see a Best Seller product in their search results, we obtained a sample of $n = 299$ participants ($M_{age} = 42$ years; $Female = 58\%$; $M_{duration} = 8$ min 23 sec).

Table 6 presents descriptive statistics as well as model-free results that indicate more pronounced differences in participant behavior between the two experimental groups compared to experiment 2. While we do not find significant differences in the total number of clicks and add-to-carts in our sample, χ^2-tests show significant differences in the likelihood of clicking and adding-to-cart for Best Seller products across experimental conditions.

---

[14] While the instructions for our study stated these terms, the winners were free to choose between the announced lottery prize and a £60 bonus payment via Prolific. This choice was not disclosed to other study participants.

Table 6. Descriptive Statistics and Model Free Results from Experiment 3

	Best Seller Visible		Best Seller Masked		Test statistic (p-value)
	$M (\sigma)$	$[min; max]$	$M (\sigma)$	$[min; max]$	
Views	19.40 (8.10)	[4;59]	20.40 (10)	[4;69]	$W = 10782$ (0.29)
Clicks	1.48 (1.09)	[1;8]	1.46 (1.27)	[1;11]	$W = 11654$ (0.20)
Time-to-cart (in sec)	238.00 (1769)	[8.94;21661]	95.30 (113)	[11.4;1104]	$W = 11262$ (0.45)
Best Seller: Clicks	0.17	-	0.07	-	$\chi^2 = 8.21$ (< 0.01)
Best Seller: Add-to-carts	0.15	-	0.05	-	$\chi^2 = 7.37$ (0.01)
Observations	149	149	150	150	299

Notes. We test mean differences in views, clicks, and time-to-cart between experimental conditions using Mann-Whitney tests, and badge-specific differences using Chi-Squared tests.

4.4.2   Model Results

We report the regression results for the click behavior model in the first two columns of Table 7. Masking the Best Seller badge yields insignificant coefficients in Models I and II. However, Model II shows a noticeable, though not statistically significant, increase in the coefficient.

The coefficients on the Best Seller product variable are insignificant in Models I and II. However, the interaction term between the Best Seller badge being masked and Best Seller product status in Model II yields a significant negative effect. This suggests a positive effect of the visual cue of the Best Seller badge.

Table 7. Regression Results for Experiment 3

Model:	I	II	III	IV
Dependent variable:	**Click**	**Click**	**Add-to-Cart**	**Add-to-Cart**
Constant	-6.455***	-6.516***	-7.838***	-7.907***
	(0.882)	(0.883)	(0.998)	(0.999)
Best Seller masked	0.015	0.118	0.016	0.130**
	(0.077)	(0.081)	(0.037)	(0.053)
Average rating	0.093***	0.093***	0.116***	0.116***
	(0.020)	(0.0197)	(0.022)	(0.022)
Number of ratings	4×10^{-5}*	4×10^{-5}*	4×10^{-5}	4×10^{-5}
	(2×10^{-5})	(2×10^{-5})	(3×10^{-5})	(3×10^{-5})
Position	-0.017**	-0.017**	-0.007	-0.007
	(0.008)	(0.008)	(0.009)	(0.009)
Price	3×10^{-5}***	3×10^{-5}***	3×10^{-5}***	3×10^{-5}***
	(1×10^{-5})	(1×10^{-5})	(1×10^{-5})	(1×10^{-5})
Best Seller product	-0.044	0.451	0.116	0.624*
	(0.241)	(0.283)	(0.286)	(0.327)
Best Seller masked × Best Seller product		-1.202***		-1.253***
		(0.408)		(0.464)
Observations	5,072	5,072	5,072	5,072
Log-Likelihood	-1,335.00	-1330.00	-1,114.00	-1,110.00
Pseudo R^2	0.015	0.018	0.015	0.019

Notes. Dependent variables: click & add-to-cart. Clustered standard errors (by user ID) in parentheses.
*** $p < 0.01$, ** $p < 0.05$, * $p < 0.1$

The last two columns of Table 7 report the regression results for the add-to-cart model. In Model III, neither the coefficient for Best Seller visibility nor the coefficient indicating a Best Seller product are significant. Model IV yields a significant and negative interaction between badge masking and the Best Seller product status. Thus, while the Best Seller badge itself increases the likelihood that a participant will add the Best Seller product to their cart, masking the badge significantly reduces this likelihood, suggesting that the visual cue plays a viable role in reinforcing the attractiveness of the product. Finally, we examine the effect of the Best Seller badge on participants' time-to-cart. The analysis does not show a statistically significant effect. Detailed regression results are added in Appendix C.

4.4.3   Discussion

In contrast to experiment 1, displaying the Best Seller badge in isolation consistently increases the likelihood that participants will click on or add Best Seller products to their carts. This finding supports the notion of a potential trade-off between the different badges in search environments with multiple badges, where the information load on consumers is higher. For example, consumers may prefer platform endorsements to popularity recommendations in search environments with higher information density, following a heuristic that the platform may be more credible or objective in its endorsement. However, in the absence of other badges, popularity information in the form of a Best Seller badge may serve as social proof (Cialdini 2009), which may be particularly effective in the context of functional products such as toasters (Steinhart et al. 2014).

5   General Discussion

Digital platforms such as Amazon use a variety of product badges, each with different implications for consumer behavior. We examine the impact of platform-controlled product badges on consumer search and choice behavior and find that the number and type of badges displayed can differentially affect consumer decision making.

In general, masking badges reduces the likelihood of product clicks, suggesting a reduction in the consideration set size. This effect is evident for platform-endorsed badges, suggesting that salient visual cues significantly influence consumer choice. An interesting exception occurs with popularity badges when presented alongside other badges in a multi-badge environment. Masking all badges increases the likelihood that consumers will click the product that received the popularity badge. Therefore, our results suggest that consumers may respond differently to platform-based endorsements versus popularity-based badges. One possible explanation for these effects is that badges help reduce search costs, providing a heuristic that simplifies consumer decision making (Ursu 2018).

However, platform endorsement badges do not significantly affect consumer behavior in a single-badge environment and controlling for product and search characteristics. This may be due to the streamlined search environment in the experimental studies, which limited other badge information and thus may have reduced the need for heuristics (Malhotra 1982).

In contrast, popularity badges increased choice in a single-badge environment, suggesting that there may be a trade-off between platform endorsement and popularity badges in multi-badge environments. This effect may be more pronounced in the absence of other badges, with popularity badges serving as social proof (Cialdini 2009).

5.1   Theoretical Implications

Our findings have important theoretical implications, suggesting that while a single badge may streamline certain participant interactions, it lacks the broader impact on participant engagement and decision making that is seen with multiple badge types or more complex recommender systems. Our findings point to a complex interplay of the effects of individual badges on consumer behavior, which not only can change the magnitude of their effect when displayed together, but also potentially reverse the direction of their effect. This suggests that models of consumer choice on digital platforms should account for the influence of and the interactions between different types of product badges.

Furthermore, as one of the first to develop a tool specifically designed to study consumer behavior in field settings, our extension provides a unique opportunity to study these dynamics in real-world settings (cf. Farronato et al. (2023)). This new tool opens possibilities for studying how digital platforms can refine consumer interactions through the strategic use of product badges.

5.2   Managerial and Public Policy Implications

From a managerial standpoint, our research shows that product badges are a cost-effective supplement to complex recommender systems and an effective way to improve the consumer experience. These visual cues can effectively guide consumers through search environments, improving the overall ease of product discovery. This insight can be particularly valuable for digital platforms looking to integrate product badges into search environments in a meaningful way.

Digital market regulation needs to consider badges as relevant design elements beyond search rankings. Due to their significant impact on consumer perception and decision making, product badges should be included in regulatory considerations to promote fairness and transparency in online marketplaces. This is especially true for platform-controlled product badges, such as the platform endorsement and popularity badges. Our findings are informative for potential regulatory policies that restrict the use of product badges, and suggest that badges may distort consumer choice by highlighting the visibility and attractiveness of certain products regardless of their quality or fit with consumer preferences. This suggests that unchecked use of product badges could lead to biased marketplaces where certain products are unfairly advantaged.

Our findings point to the need for digital platform guidelines that reveal the criteria for awarding product badges. In the absence of transparency, badges may be used in a biased manner, going beyond mere signals of product quality. This could lead to consumer misinformation and manipulation of purchasing behavior, which is contrary to the concept of informing consumers and promoting fair competition. Therefore, regulatory frameworks and digital platform policies need to enforce standards for badge assignment to ensure that product badges reflect product quality.

On the other hand, both sellers and consumers can benefit from the use of product badges. For sellers, badges can increase the visibility of their products, potentially leading to increased sales. They act as recommendations, highlighting the quality or popularity of a product. Products with badges attract more attention on digital platforms when competing with other sellers. For consumers, badges can simplify the decision-making process by signaling which products are recommended or popular among other customers. As a result, badges can save consumers time and effort when selecting from multiple products on digital platforms.

5.3   Limitations and Future Research

We have to acknowledge the limitations of our study and experimental paradigm, which may affect the interpretation and generalizability of our findings. First, we focus on Amazon because of its dominant position in many markets. However, future research may explore similar product badges on other platforms. Moreover, while Amazon's prominence may increase consumer trust in its endorsements, our findings may not fully generalize to smaller platforms. Second, without precise information about Amazon's platform endorsement allocation mechanism, potential interdependencies between badge types require further investigation to be fully understood. Third, our field experiments relied on an experimental participant pool with informed consent.

Several avenues for future research could extend the findings of our research. One important area of research is to identify the underlying mechanisms that drive the observed consumer behavior. Investigating how search costs affect consumer interactions with product badges may reveal why certain badge configurations are more effective than others. Another potential line of research is to study the generalizability of our findings from Amazon's platform to other digital platforms, especially those that target different product categories. By testing the generalizability of the findings, researchers can determine the broader applicability of product badge strategies across different online marketplaces. Furthermore, beyond online retailing, future research could consider settings such as review sites like TripAdvisor and Yelp, streaming platforms, or search engines. These platforms often use visual indicators similar to product badges, and studying their impact on consumer behavior could reveal common patterns or distinct differences. In addition, varying search terms and observing how they influence consumer behavior with these badges would contribute to a deeper understanding of their role in guiding consumer choices.

Previous research has focused primarily on product badges that appear to be beneficial to sellers. However, there are also badges that warn consumers, such as the "Frequently Returned Items Badge" on Amazon US.[15] This badge is given to products with high return rates compared to similar products in the same category. Such warning badges can serve as indicators for consumers, alerting them to potential problems with a product before they make a purchase. Future research could examine the impact of these warning badges on consumer behavior and decision making. Specifically, it would be valuable to analyze how these types of product badges affect overall consumer trust and how they affect perceptions of the product and the seller.

To summarize, our findings highlight the complex dynamics between different types of badges and their effects on consumer behavior. Further research is needed to unravel the underlying mechanisms driving these effects and to explore the broader implications for e-commerce platforms and consumer decision making.

---

[15] https://ecommercenurse.com/what-is-the-frequently-returned-items-badge-on-amazon-and-how-to-avoid-being-awarded-one/.

Appendix

Appendix A: Literature Overview

Table A1 provides an overview of recent literature on platform conduct and regulation. As evidenced by this selection, the majority of research within this field focuses on the effects of vertical integration of platforms. Platform design elements, such as recommendations or search rankings, have been examined to a lesser degree. However, badges, constituting another salient platform design feature, have received little scholarly attention within this field. In addition, most studies have employed a formal-analytical model to investigate their respective research questions, limiting the external validity of their results.

Table A2 provides an overview of literature on different badge types (see Section 2: Product Badges as Platform Design Tools in the main paper for a more detailed classification of badge types). As outlined in Table A2, only few studies employ experiments, with even less research conducted in field settings.

Table A1. Overview of Literature on Platform Conduct and Regulation

Study	Focus	Platform Instrument	Research Method
Anderson and Bedre-Defolie 2021	Vertical integration / self-preferencing	Fees and prices of own products	Formal-analytical model
Bar-Isaac and Shelegia 2022	Platform design	Fees and algorithmic steering	Formal-analytical model
Bisceglia and Padilla 2023	Vertical integration / seller cooperation	Fees and prices of own products	Formal-analytical model
Calvano et al. 2023	Platform design	Recommender systems	Formal-analytical model
Chen and Tsai 2023	Platform design	Recommendations	Observational data
Derakhshan et al. 2022	Platform design	Search rankings	Formal-analytical model
Dinerstein et al. 2018	Platform design	Search process	Observational data & formal-analytical model
Etro 2021a	Platform competition	Platform business model	Formal-analytical model
Etro 2021b	Vertical integration	Market entry	Formal-analytical model
Etro 2023	Vertical integration	Fees	Formal-analytical model
Farronato et al. 2023	Vertical integration / self-preferencing	Search rankings	Experiment
Gutierrez 2021	Vertical integration / self-preferencing	Fees	Formal-analytical model
Hagiu et al. 2022	Vertical integration / self-preferencing	Vertical integration	Formal-analytical model
Iyengar et al. 2023	Platform design (services)	Seller fulfillment	Formal-analytical model
Lam 2023	Platform design	Search rankings	Formal-analytical model

Study	Focus	Platform Instrument	Research Method
Lee and Musolff 2023	Platform design	Recommendations	Formal-analytical model
Long and Amaldoss 2024	Vertical integration / self-preferencing	Sponsored Advertising	Formal-analytical model
Padilla et al. 2022	Vertical integration / self-preferencing	Foreclosure	Formal-analytical model
Shopova 2023	Vertical integration / self-preferencing	Vertical integration	Formal-analytical model
Zennyo 2022	Vertical integration / self-preferencing	Search results	Formal-analytical model

Table A2. Overview of Literature on the Effects of Various Type of Product Badges

Study	Type of Badges	Research Method
Aguiar and Waldfogel 2018	Platform endorsement	Panel data & instrumental variables
Bairathi et al. 2022	Platform endorsement	Field experiment
Cheng et al. 2020	Platform endorsement	Panel data
Cui and Shin 2018	Availability-related	Formal-analytical model
Cui et al. 2019	Availability-related	Field experiment
Dewan et al. 2023	Platform endorsement	Difference-in-difference
Eisenbeiss et al. 2015	Price-related	Experiments
Elfenbein et al. 2015	Platform endorsement	Matching
Ghiassaleh et al. 2020	Popularity-related	Experiments
Ghose and Yang 2009	Advertising-related	Formal-analytical model
Goodman et al. 2013	Popularity-related	Experiments
Hui et al. 2016	Platform endorsement	Difference-in-difference
Hukal et al. 2020	Platform endorsement	Mixed methods
Mishra et al. 2023	Platform endorsement	Regression Discontinuity Design
Rietveld et al. 2021	Platform endorsement	Difference-in-difference
Saeedi 2019	Platform endorsement	Formal-analytical model
Wang and Qiu 2024	Platform endorsement	Formal-analytical model

Appendix B: Study of Badge Prevalence

Table B1 details all search terms used in our study on badge prevalence on Amazon (see Section 3 in paper for a detailed description of the data collection process). All search terms were generated using OpenAI's ChatGPT. Duplicates were manually removed and replaced. Table B2 depicts the descriptive statistics for badge prevalence.

Table B1. Exemplary Search Terms Used in the Data Collection Process for Badge Prevalence

Category	Example Search Terms
Beauty	aftershave for men, foot cream, hair dye, eye cream dark circles, manicure kit, body butter, tanning lotion, foundation makeup, facial roller, hair volumizer spray, rosehip oil, essential oils set, retinol serum, bath bombs, makeup sponge
Books	space exploration, archaeology, memoirs, cultural studies, historical fiction, suspense thrillers, biography, psychology, true crime, war stories, play scripts, educational, modern history, home decor books, craftsmanship
Clothing, Shoes & Jewelry	sports bras, kids' sneakers, diamond bracelets, cowboy boots, men's suits, floral dresses, summer hats, pearl necklaces, boots, satchel bags, sneakers, beach dresses, handbags, evening gowns, women's dresses
Computer	dual monitor stand, graphics card, hard drive, laptop stand, desktop organizer, macbook air, notebook cooler, gaming mouse pad, touchscreen monitor, streaming camera, ssd enclosure, cable management, printer, windows laptop, memory card reader
Electronics	action camera, smart lock, desktop pc, cd player, cordless mouse, camera lens, printers, 3d printer, home theater system, thermostat, wireless charger, portable charger, wireless printer, external hard drive, vr headset
Grocery	organic rice, raw honey, gourmet rice, gourmet coffee blends, specialty sugars, ancient grains, dried fruits, vegan sausages, quinoa products, vegan cookies, pasta sauces, gluten-free flours, protein bars, organic tea, vegan pastas

Category	Example Search Terms
Health	potty training seat, weight scale, organic hand soaps, baby safety gates, baby bibs, power toothbrush, menstrual cups, multivitamin for women, baby carriers, pain killers, herbal teas, essential oils, facial tissue, natural remedies, glucose meter
Home & Kitchen	coffee maker, storage shelves, wall decals, grill pan, bar stools, kitchen island, bedspread, glassware, throw pillows, bathroom accessories, rugs, cake stand, floor lamp, wine opener, can opener
Sports & Outdoor	roller skates, gym supplements, badminton shuttlecock, mountain bike, climbing gear, running shoes, hiking boots, snowboard, rugby ball, bicycle, camping chair, tennis racket, camping tent, table tennis paddle, gym bag
Toys & Games	novelty toys, puzzles, miniature playsets, wooden toys, outdoor toys, drawing kits, learning toys, spinning tops, skateboards, video games, clay modeling, role play costumes, magic cubes, robotic toys, sports toys

Table B2. Descriptive Statistics for Badge Prevalence

	Amazon's Choice (AC)	Products in Product Categories With AC (AC excl.)	Best Seller (BS)	Products in Product Categories With Best Seller (BS excl.)	All Products
Mean price	**40.64**	**49.34**	**41.13**	**47.05**	**47.42**
Vendor: Amazon	46.05	59.66	51.67	53.96	54.44
Vendor: Other	37.24	46.43	35.85	44.93	45.20
Mean rating	**4.45**	**4.35**	**4.43**	**4.35**	**4.35**
Vendor: Amazon	4.50	4.43	4.49	4.43	4.44
Vendor: Other	4.42	4.33	4.40	4.32	4.32
Mean rank	**11.40**	**34.50**	**24.20**	**33.80**	**33.20**
Vendor: Amazon	9.67	33.20	22.40	30.80	30.10
Vendor: Other	12.50	34.90	25.00	34.60	34.10
No. of products	**3,055**	**174,716**	**7,292**	**201,421**	**231,547**
Vendor: Amazon	1,176	37,619	2,413	46,135	54,475
Vendor: Other	1,879	137,097	4,879	155,286	177,072

Notes. Comparison of mean prices, ratings, and ranks, and prevalence of products (not) labeled as Amazon's Choice and Best Seller.

Figures B1 and B2 display the search rank distribution by badge (product information) type, accounting for different display formats. Specifically, a search grid contains multiple search results per row, resulting in a far higher number of organic search results than contained in search lists. As outlined in section 3 of the main paper, the search rank distributions per badge type generally follow the same patterns across these two display formats.

Figure B1. Search Rank Distribution by Badge Type (per Search Term, Display Format: Grid)

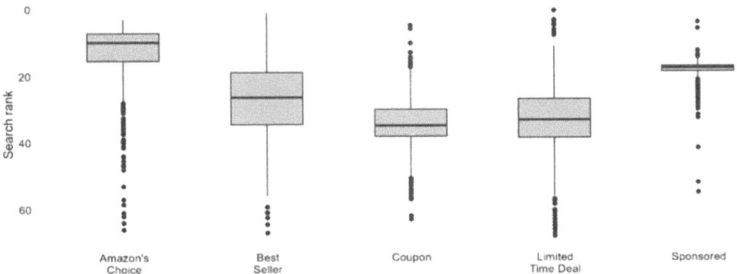

Figure B2. Search Rank Distribution by Badge Type (per Search Term, Display Format: List)

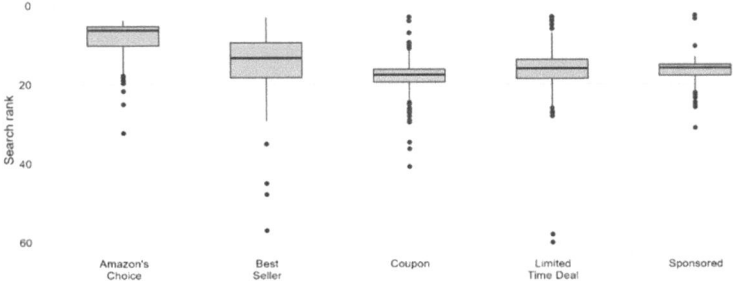

Appendix C: Experimental Studies

Table C1 displays regression results with respect to users' time-to-cart, i.e., the time elapsed between a user's initial access to the Amazon search results page for the keyword *toaster* and their initial add-to-cart event during experiment 1. As evidenced by these results, the effect of masking badges on users' time-to-cart is insignificant when accounting for other user characteristics.

Table C1. Regression Results for Experiment 1

Model:	I	II
Dependent Variable:	**Time-to-Cart**	**Time-to-Cart**
Constant	4.097***	3.566***
	(0.072)	(0.248)
Badges masked	-0.003*	-0.043
	(0.103)	(0.098)
User age		0.013***
		(0.004)
User gender		-0.193*
		(0.100)
Amazon usage: Less than monthly		0.002
		(0.203)
Amazon usage: Monthly		0.414*
		(0.2421)
Amazon usage: Weekly		-0.470
		(0.538)
Observations	210	210
R^2	0.000	0.123

Notes. Dependent variable: time-to-cart. Robust standard errors in parentheses.
*** $p < 0.01$, ** $p < 0.05$, * $p < 0.1$.

Table C2 displays regression results with respect to users' time-to-cart, i.e., the time elapsed between a user's initial access to the Amazon search results page for the keyword *toaster* and their initial add-to-cart event during experiment 2. As evidenced by these results, the effect of masking badges on users' time-to-cart is insignificant when accounting for other user characteristics.

Table C2. Regression Results for Experiment 2

Model:	I	II
Dependent Variable:	**Time-to-Cart**	**Time-to-Cart**
Constant	4.244***	3.692***
	(0.055)	(0.242)
Treated	-0.030	-0.040
	(0.077)	(0.075)
User age		0.012***
		(0.003)
User gender		-0.178**
		(0.075)
Amazon usage: Never		1.360**
		(0.691)
Amazon usage: Less than monthly		0.671***
		(0.209)
Amazon usage: Monthly		0.419**
		(0.190)
Amazon usage: Weekly		0.294
		(0.187)
Observations	320	319
R^2	0.001	0.095

Notes. Dependent variable: time-to-cart. Robust standard errors in parentheses. *** $p < 0.01$, ** $p < 0.05$, * $p < 0.1$.

Table C3 displays regression results with respect to users' time-to-cart, i.e., the time elapsed between a user's initial access to the Amazon search results page for the keyword *toaster* and their initial add-to-cart event during experiment 3. As evidenced by these results, the effect of masking badges on users' time-to-cart is insignificant when accounting for other user characteristics.

Table C3. Regression Results for Experiment 3

Model:	I	II
Dependent Variable:	**Time-to-Cart**	**Time-to-Cart**
Constant	4.305***	3.717***
	(0.064)	(0.263)
Treated	-0.038	-0.036
	(0.090)	(0.090)
User age		0.012***
		(0.003)
User gender		-0.041***
		(0.093)
Amazon usage: Never		0.326
		(0.385)
Amazon usage: Less than monthly		0.208***
		(0.209)
Amazon usage: Monthly		0.151**
		(0.186)
Amazon usage: Weekly		0.130*
		(0.181)
Observations	299	298
R^2	0.001	0.049

Notes. Dependent variable: time-to-cart. Robust standard errors in parentheses.
*** $p < 0.01$, ** $p < 0.05$, * $p < 0.1$.

References

Aguiar L, Waldfogel J (2018) Platforms, promotion, and product discovery: Evidence from Spotify playlists. *National Bureau of Economic Research Working Paper* No. 24713.

Allcott H, Gentzkow M, Song L (2022) Digital addiction. *American Economic Review*. 112(7):2424–2463.

Anderson S, Bedre-Defolie Ö (2021) Hybrid platform model, C.E.P.R. Discussion Papers.

Atkinson L, Rosenthal S (2014) Signaling the green sell: The influence of eco-label source, argument specificity, and product involvement on consumer trust. *Journal of Advertising*. 43(1):33–45.

Bairathi M, Zhang X, Lambrecht A (2022) The value of platform endorsement. SSRN: https://ssrn.com/abstract=4144605.

Bar-Isaac H, Shelegia S (2022) Monetizing Steering, C.E.P.R. Discussion Papers.

Bisceglia M, Padilla J (2023) On sellers' cooperation in hybrid marketplaces. *Journal of Economics & Management Strategy*. 32(1):207–222.

Blake T, Nosko C, Tadelis S (2015) Consumer heterogeneity and paid search effectiveness: A large-scale field experiment. *Econometrica*. 83(1):155–174.

Blattberg RC, Briesch R, Fox EJ (1995) How promotions work. *Marketing Science*. 14(3):122-132.

Broniarczyk SM, Griffin JG (2014) Decision difficulty in the age of consumer empowerment. *Journal of Consumer Psychology*. 24(4):608–625.

Brynjolfsson E, Hu Y, Rahman MS (2009) Battle of the retail channels: How product selection and geography drive cross-channel competition. *Management Science*. 55(11):1755–1765.

Cai H, Chen Y, Fang H (2009) Observational learning: Evidence from a randomized natural field experiment. *American Economic Review*. 99(3):864–882.

Calvano E, Calzolari G, Denicolò V, Pastorello S (2023) Artificial intelligence, algorithmic recommendations and competition. SSRN: https://ssrn.com/abstract=4448010.

Cameron AC, Miller DL (2015) A practitioner's guide to cluster-robust inference. *Journal of Human Resources*. 50(2):317–372.

Carare O (2012) The impact of bestseller rank on demand: Evidence from the app market. *International Economic Review*. 53(3):717–742.

Chen N, Tsai H-T (2023) Steering via algorithmic recommendations. SSRN: https://ssrn.com/abstract=3500407.

Cheng HK, Fan W, Guo P, Huang H, Qiu L (2020) Can "gold medal" online sellers earn gold? The impact of reputation badges on sales. *Journal of Management Information Systems.* 37(4):1099–1127.

Cialdini RB (2009) *Influence. Science and Practice,* 5th ed. (Pearson Education, Harlow).

Cui R, Li M, Li Q (2020) Value of high-quality logistics: Evidence from a clash between SF Express and Alibaba. *Management Science.* 66(9):3879–3902.

Cui R, Shin H (2018) Sharing aggregate inventory information with customers: Strategic cross-selling and shortage reduction. *Management Science.* 64(1):381–400.

Cui R, Zhang DJ, Bassamboo A (2019) Learning from inventory availability information: Evidence from field experiments on Amazon. *Management Science.* 65(3):1216–1235.

Dai W, Kim H, Luca M (2023) Frontiers: Which firms gain from digital advertising? Evidence from a field experiment. *Marketing Science.* 42(3):429–439.

Derakhshan M, Golrezaei N, Manshadi V, Mirrokni V (2022) Product Ranking on Online Platforms. *Management Science.* 68(6):4024–4041.

Dewan S, Kim J, Nian T (2023) Economic impacts of platform-endorsed quality certification: Evidence from Airbnb. *MIS Quarterly.* 47(3):1353–1368.

Dinerstein M, Einav L, Levin J, Sundaresan N (2018) Consumer price search and platform design in Internet commerce. *American Economic Review.* 108(7):1820–1859.

Eisenbeiss M, Wilken R, Skiera B, Cornelissen M (2015) What makes deal-of-the-day promotions really effective? The interplay of discount and time constraint with product type. *International Journal of Research in Marketing.* 32(4):387–397.

Elfenbein DW, Fisman R, McManus B (2015) Market structure, reputation, and the value of quality certification. *American Economic Journal: Microeconomics.* 7(4):83–108.

Etro F (2021a) Device-funded vs ad-funded platforms. *International Journal of Industrial Organization.* 75:102711.

Etro F (2021b) Product selection in online marketplaces. *Journal of Economics & Management Strategy.* 30(3):614–637.

Etro F (2023) Hybrid marketplaces with free entry of sellers. *Review of Industrial Organization*. 62(2):119–148.

Farronato C, Fradkin A, Karr C (2024) Webmunk: A new tool for studying online behavior and digital platforms. *National Bureau of Economic Research Working Paper* No. 32694.

Farronato C, Fradkin A, MacKay A (2023) Self-preferencing at Amazon: Evidence from search rankings. *AEA Papers and Proceedings*. 113: 239–43.

Friestad M, Wright P (1994) The persuasion knowledge model: How people cope with persuasion attempts. *Journal of Consumer Research*. 21(1):1–31.

Ghiassaleh A, Kocher B, Czellar S (2020) Best Seller!? Unintended negative consequences of popularity signs on consumer choice behavior. *International Journal of Research in Marketing*. 37(4):805–820.

Ghose A, Yang S (2009) An empirical analysis of search engine advertising: Sponsored search in electronic markets. *Management Science*. 55(10):1605–1622.

Goodman JK, Broniarczyk SM, Griffin JG, McAlister L (2013) Help or hinder? When recommendation signage expands consideration sets and heightens decision difficulty. *Journal of Consumer Psychology*. 23(2):165–174.

Gutierrez G (2021) The welfare consequences of regulating Amazon. SSRN: https://ssrn.com/abstract=3965566.

Hagiu A, Teh T-H, Wright J (2022) Should platforms be allowed to sell on their own marketplaces? *The RAND Journal of Economics*. 53(2):297–327.

Harter A, Stich L, Spann M (2024) The effect of delivery time on repurchase behavior in quick commerce. *Journal of Service Research*. Forthcoming.

Häubl G, Trifts V (2000) Consumer decision making in online shopping environments: The effects of interactive decision aids. *Marketing Science*. 19(1):4–21.

Honka E, Seiler S, Ursu R (2024) Consumer search: What can we learn from pre-purchase data? *Journal of Retailing*. 100(1):114–129.

Hui X, Saeedi M, Shen Z, Sundaresan N (2016) Reputation and regulations: Evidence from eBay. *Management Science*. 62(12):3604–3616.

Hukal P, Henfridsson O, Shaikh M, Parker G (2020) Platform signaling for generating platform content. *MIS Quarterly*. 44(3):1177–1205.

Inman JJ, Peter AC, Raghubir P (1997) Framing the deal: The role of restrictions in accentuating deal value. *Journal of Consumer Research*. 24(1):68–79.

Iyengar G, Ma Y, Rivera T, Saleh F, Sethuraman J (2023) The distributional effects of 'Fulfilled By Amazon' (FBA). SSRN: https://ssrn.com/abstract=4365855.

Iyengar SS, Lepper MR (2000) When choice is demotivating: Can one desire too much of a good thing? *Journal of Personality and Social Psychology.* 79(6):995–1006.

Jerath K, Ma L, Park Y-H, Srinivasan K (2011) A "position paradox" in sponsored search auctions. *Marketing Science.* 30(4):612–627.

Kim JB, Albuquerque P, Bronnenberg BJ (2010) Online demand under limited consumer search. *Marketing Science.* 29(6):1001–1023.

Kumar P, Kalwani MU, Dada M (1997) The impact of waiting time guarantees on customers' waiting experiences. *Marketing Science.* 16(4):295–314.

Lam HT (2023) Platform search design and market power. Available at: https://www.dropbox.com/s/y1t4gdph322ln3q/Lam_JMP_Platform_Sea rch_Design.pdf.

Lee KH, Musolff L (2023) Entry into two-sided markets shaped by platform-guided search.

Long F, Amaldoss W (2024) Self-preferencing in e-commerce marketplaces: The role of sponsored advertising and private labels. *Marketing Science.* Forthcoming.

Malhotra NK (1982) Information load and consumer decision making. *Journal of Consumer Research.* 8(4):419.

Mishra R, Huang G, Kalwani M (2023) The Value of Reputation Badges for Sellers in the Age of Ratings and Review: An Empirical Study of Airbnb's Superhost Program. SSRN: https://ssrn.com/abstract=4527337.

Padilla J, Perkins J, Piccolo S (2022) Self-Preferencing in Markets with Vertically Integrated Gatekeeper Platforms. *The Journal of Industrial Economics.* 70(2):371–395.

Park S, Xie M, Xie J (2023) Frontiers: Framing price increase as discount: A new manipulation of reference price. *Marketing Science.* 42(1):37–47.

Peng J, Liang C (2023) On the differences between view-based and purchase-based recommender systems. *MIS Quarterly.* 47(2):875–900.

Rietveld J, Schilling MA (2021) Platform competition: A systematic and interdisciplinary review of the literature. *Journal of Management.* 47(6):1528–1563.

Rietveld J, Schilling MA, Bellavitis C (2019) Platform strategy: Managing ecosystem value through selective promotion of complements. *Organization Science*. 30(6):1232–1251.

Rietveld J, Seamans R, Meggiorin K (2021) Market orchestrators: The effects of certification on platforms and their complementors. *Strategy Science*. 6(3):244–264.

Saeedi M (2019) Reputation and adverse selection: theory and evidence from eBay. *The RAND Journal of Economics*. 50(4):822–853.

Salganik MJ, Dodds PS, Watts DJ (2006) Experimental study of inequality and unpredictability in an artificial cultural market. *Science (New York, N.Y.)*. 311(5762):854–856.

Shopova R (2023) Private labels in marketplaces. *International Journal of Industrial Organization*. 89:102949.

Steinhart Y, Kamins M, Mazursky D, Noy A (2014) Effects of product type and contextual cues on eliciting naive theories of popularity and exclusivity. *Journal of Consumer Psychology*. 24(4):472–483.

Tucker C, Zhang J (2011) How does popularity information affect choices? A field experiment. *Management Science*. 57(5):828–842.

Ursu RM (2018) The power of rankings: Quantifying the effect of rankings on online consumer search and purchase decisions. *Marketing Science*. 37(4):530–552.

Wang R, Qiu Y (2024) Dual Role and Product Featuring Strategy of Digital Platform. *Marketing Science*. Forthcoming.

Weitzman ML (1979) Optimal search for the best alternative. *Econometrica*. 47(3):641.

Wu L, Lee C (2016) Limited edition for me and Best Seller for you: The impact of scarcity versus popularity cues on self versus other-purchase behavior. *Journal of Retailing*. 92(4):486–499.

Yang LW, Aggarwal P (2019) No small matter: How company size affects consumer expectations and evaluations. *Journal of Consumer Research*. 45(6):1369–1384.

Yang S, Lu S, Lu X (2014) Modeling competition and its impact on paid-search advertising. *Marketing Science*. 33(1):134–153.

Zennyo Y (2022) Platform Encroachment and Own-Content Bias. *The Journal of Industrial Economics*. 70(3):684–710.

Conclusion

Recommender systems (RSs) are essential tools that support consumers in discovering and navigating online content catalogs, enhancing the online shopping experience (Häubl and Trifts 2000). However, this dissertation provides insights into how RSs influence consumer behavior and potentially affect decision-making. Focusing on three RS dimensions of item selection, ranking and display, this research analyzes how each dimension induces behavioral biases and can influence consumer behavior.

Despite the growing literature on RS research, field experiments in this area remain sparse. To address this gap, we conducted field experiments to test and empirically validate consumer behavior concepts. On one hand, our findings validate insights from studies supported by laboratory experiments, confirming them in real-world contexts. On the other hand, we contribute to the RS literature by offering new insights into the roles of assimilation and contrast effects and the influence of product badges on consumer behavior within RSs. Additionally, the dissertation demonstrates how modern software tools can be leveraged to facilitate field experiments, providing a framework for future empirical research in real-world settings. In the following sections, we summarize the main findings of each article, discuss their theoretical and managerial implications, and propose avenues for future research.

1   Summary of Results

The first article of this dissertation is a systematic literature review on behavioral biases in RSs and provides the foundation for the dissertation. We identify and analyze 43 articles from 26 journals and five conference proceedings. Descriptive results show that most publications are from the research discipline of information systems (IS), followed by marketing. According to DellaVigna's (2009) framework, ten different biases are identified and categorized based on their influence on nonstandard preferences, beliefs and decision-making. The literature review further analyzes the biases induced by three key RS dimensions: item quantity and selection, item ranking, and explanation and reviews. It provides an overview of how each dimension induces behavioral biases. Most of the identified articles focus on nonstandard decision-making, illustrating the widespread impact of RSs on altering consumer choices beyond rational decision-making. Furthermore, only nine out of the 43 identified studies utilize field experiments. The most common research methods employed in these studies are laboratory experiments or secondary data analysis of publicly available observational data.

The second article investigates the influence of contextual similarity on user behavior within RSs in retail e-commerce. Through a field experiment, the study examines how contextual similarities between a currently inspected product and recommendations affect consumer click behavior. The findings reveal that visual similarity significantly increases click-through rates (CTRs), suggesting that users are more likely to engage with recommendations that resemble what they are currently viewing. This phenomenon can be explained through assimilation effects (Bless and Schwarz 2010), a behavioral bias in which consumers are inclined to accept recommendations that are perceived as similar to the focal product. Our findings challenge the emphasis on diversity and serendipity in RSs, indicating that users prefer product recommendations that align more closely with the product they are inspecting. Furthermore, the study offers practical insights for improving RS design by prioritizing similarity over diversity in product recommendations, particularly in retail e-commerce.

Building upon the second article, the third article analyzes the impact of position and contrast effects on user decision-making within RSs. Through a field experiment, the study explores how the placement of a specific focal recommendation and the degree of contrast between this item and other recommendations influence CTRs. The results reveal that contrary to common assumptions, placing a focal item in the second or third position in a list rather than at the top increases its acceptance rate. This effect can be attributed to position bias

(Häubl et al. 2010, Guo et al. 2023), a behavioral bias where users are inclined to select items placed in non-primary positions. These positions allow for better comparison with previously viewed items, enhancing their attractiveness. A higher visual contrast between a focal product and other recommendations increases the CTR. This can be explained through contrast effects (Bless and Schwarz 2010), where the distinctiveness of a focal product relative to surrounding items makes it stand out more and appear more appealing. This effect is even more pronounced when the surrounding recommendations are less relevant. These findings challenge the notion that top-ranked recommendations are always the most effective and emphasize the importance of strategically positioning and contrasting recommendations to optimize user engagement in RSs.

The fourth article examines the impact of product badges on consumer search and decision-making behavior (Cheng et al. 2020). The study finds that the number and type of badges displayed can significantly influence consumer choices. In general, masking badges reduces the likelihood of product clicks, suggesting a decrease in the size of consumers' consideration sets (CSs). This effect is particularly pronounced for platform-endorsed badges, indicating that prominent visual cues are critical in guiding consumer decisions. However, an exception arises with popularity badges: when these badges are masked, consumers are more likely to click on the associated products. This suggests that consumers may react differently to platform-based endorsements than popularity-based recommendations. One possible explanation for these findings is that badges function as heuristics, reducing search costs by simplifying decision-making processes.

2 Implications and Avenues for Future Research

The results of this dissertation allow us to derive several theoretical and managerial implications as well as avenues for future research.

2.1   Theoretical Implications

Article 1 highlights a critical gap in RS research: the scarcity of field experiments. Much of the existing literature relies on laboratory experiments and publicly available observational data, such as LastFM[1] (Wei et al. 2022) or MovieLens[2] (Bollen et al. 2010, Yang et al. 2013, Willemsen et al. 2016, Su et al. 2023). This reliance on a few popular datasets raises concerns about the generalizability of findings, as some insights are potentially artifacts of these datasets and can not be replicated across different contexts. Our dissertation addresses this limitation by conducting field experiments, which provide high external validity and offer a more robust understanding of consumer behavior in real-world settings. Article 3 challenges widely accepted assumptions drawn from secondary data analysis, such as the preference for high-ranking recommendations (Bian et al. 2012, Melchiorre et al. 2023). Through a field experiment, the study reveals that lower rankings can lead to higher CTRs. This finding underscores the need for a broader range of data sources in RS research, particularly field experiments that validate or challenge insights derived from traditional datasets utilized in RS research. Studies that utilize publicly available RS datasets should combine several data sources and potentially enhance the validity of their findings through additional lab or field experiments (cf. Yalcin and Bilge (2022), Zhao et al. (2022))

Furthermore, Article 3 demonstrates that non-relevant recommendations can increase CTRs for certain products. This finding contradicts one of the RSs' purposes to display personalized and relevant content to consumers. Hence, the article opens up a new avenue for understanding how contrast effects can influence consumer behavior in RSs, a topic that has seen limited exploration in the literature (Häubl et al. 2010, Guo et al. 2023). Given the close connection between contrast effects and RS diversity, where diversity refers to "internal differences within parts

---

[1] http://ocelma.net/MusicRecommendationDataset/lastfm-360K.html
[2] https://grouplens.org/datasets/movielens/100k/

of an experience" (Castells et al. 2021), this perspective suggests that diversity within RSs may not only improve user satisfaction by offering a broader range of options (Zhang and Hurley 2008) but also by enhancing the appeal of certain recommendations through contrast effects. In this sense, diversity serves a dual function: it provides variety and increases the perceived value of focal items when displayed with less relevant alternatives. This understanding of diversity as both a source of variety and a mechanism for creating contrast offers a nuanced view of how diverse recommendations can affect consumer behavior. Therefore, research should integrate the dual perspective of RS diversity and recognize that it can influence user behavior and satisfaction differently (Knijnenburg et al. 2012).

As technology advances and more sophisticated software becomes available, conducting field experiments in real-world settings has become increasingly feasible. Integrating software into existing digital landscapes allows researchers to observe consumer behavior and manipulate the appearance and functionality of digital platforms. Article 4 exemplifies this approach by demonstrating how field experiments can be conducted on a digital platform without direct access to the system architecture (cf. Farronato et al. (2023)). This opens up new possibilities for RS research, enabling more nuanced insights into consumer behavior and providing a more dynamic method of testing hypotheses in natural environments. Additionally, this approach allows researchers to alter digital interfaces, offering a powerful tool for studying the effects of different RS strategies in the field.

2.2   Managerial Implications

Although RSs can serve as effective consumer tools to navigate product catalogs, this dissertation emphasizes the importance of recognizing the biases induced by RSs. While RSs can guide consumer choices, these biases can lead to suboptimal decisions and affect overall consumer satisfaction (Chen et al. 2023). Practitioners need to be mindful that user feedback, often fed back into the RS, can potentially reinforce these biases over time (Jannach et al. 2018). To mitigate such issues, applying debiasing strategies ensures that RSs lead to more balanced and accurate recommendations (Boratto et al. 2021, Chen et al. 2023).

Furthermore, this dissertation highlights that RS influences extend beyond traditional dimensions such as item selection, ranking, and explanation. Different RS dimensions have varied effects, but additional factors, like product badges, also significantly shape consumer behavior. Article 4 illustrates how product badges function as an RS dimension that can strategically influence consumer choices. By effectively leveraging product badges within RSs, digital platforms can enhance the visibility and sales of certain products. This insight could be valuable for promoting private-label items, enabling platforms to increase their market share.

Moreover, Article 3 challenges the conventional assumption that higher RS rankings always yield the best outcomes. It shows that non-primary positions can also lead to higher acceptance rates for specific products, suggesting that digital platforms can promote their branded products without necessarily placing them at the top of the recommendation list. This finding offers a more nuanced approach to RS design, allowing for subtle yet effective promotion strategies.

However, regulators and policymakers should consider these less prominent but influential factors when formulating regulations. The implications of RS design, ranking strategies, and product badges extend beyond mere consumer convenience and potentially bias consumer behavior. Recognizing the full spectrum of RS influences is essential for creating balanced and consumer-friendly digital platforms. For instance, while the EU Digital Services Act (DSA)[3] emphasizes the explainability of recommendations to users (DSA Article 27), it does not account for the nuanced benefits that certain products may gain through contrast effects, lower rankings, and the strategic use of product badges. The results from this dissertation imply that these factors should be considered to ensure that digital

---

[3] https://www.eu-digital-services-act.com/Digital_Services_Act_Article_27.html

platforms operate fairly and transparently. Expanding the scope of such regulations to include these insights would enhance consumer protection and promote fair competition in digital marketplaces.

2.3   Future Research

The dissertation leaves several avenues for future research to enhance our understanding of RS long-term effects and address some limitations.

First, the dissertation's empirical articles focus on short-term metrics such as CTRs and add-to-cart behavior. Long-term effects of RS usage are not examined, as the studies rely on short observation periods (54 days in Article 2, 14 weeks in Article 3 and session data in Article 4). This reflects a broader trend in RS research, where the emphasis is often placed on short-term engagement at the expense of long-term performance (Xue et al. 2019). Future research should prioritize understanding how RSs impact consumer behavior over extended periods, which would provide more robust insights into the sustainability and long-term effects on consumer behavior of RSs.

Second, future research should also extend beyond the commonly studied item-based collaborative filtering (IBCF) RSs, which primarily rely on purchase data. These RSs are popular in business practice and research due to their ease of implementation (Adomavicius et al. 2013, Lee and Hosanagar 2019, 2021) and are also used in this dissertation. However, recent studies suggest that both the chosen RS algorithm and the type of user data used can impact consumer behavior, such as CTRs and product selection (Peng and Liang 2023). Therefore, researchers should be precise about their applied RS algorithms and the data sources that generate the recommendations, as different approaches can lead to varying consumer responses. The availability of open-source tools, like Google's TensorFlow Recommenders[4]

---

[4] https://www.tensorflow.org/recommenders

or Microsoft-Recommenders[5], provides an opportunity to apply diverse RS models, allowing for more nuanced investigations into how different data types and RS algorithms shape consumer behavior.

Third, exploring how RSs influence the formation of CSs could also deepen our understanding of consumer decision-making (Li et al. 2022). Specifically, investigating which products users consider and how behavioral biases alter the composition of CSs would be valuable. While this dissertation primarily focuses on how biases impact consumer preferences, beliefs, and decision-making, future research could also address the implications from an item perspective and focus on the composition of consumer CSs under RS usage.

Finally, as artificial intelligence advances, its integration into RSs presents new opportunities for enhancing user experience and acceptance. Incorporating large language models into RSs can provide more sophisticated and personalized explanations for recommendations, further increasing user trust and satisfaction (Sacharidis 2020). However, the impact of AI-driven RSs, particularly regarding user transparency and long-term effectiveness, remains an open question. Future research should explore how these advanced technologies can shape the next generation of RSs and their influence on consumers and markets.

---

[5] https://microsoft-recommenders.readthedocs.io/en/latest/

References

Adomavicius G, Bockstedt JC, Curley SP, Zhang J (2013) Do recommender systems manipulate consumer preferences? A study of anchoring effects. *Information Systems Research* 24(4):956-975.

Bian J, Dong A, He X, Reddy S, Chang Y (2012) User action interpretation for online content optimization. *IEEE transactions on knowledge and data engineering* 25(9):2161-2174.

Bless H, Schwarz N (2010) Mental construal and the emergence of assimilation and contrast effects: The inclusion/exclusion model. *Advances in Experimental Social Psychology*, vol. 42 (Elsevier), 319-373.

Bollen D, Knijnenburg BP, Willemsen MC, Graus M (2010) Understanding choice overload in recommender systems. *Proceedings of the fourth ACM Conference on Recommender Systems*, 63-70.

Boratto L, Fenu G, Marras M (2021) Connecting user and item perspectives in popularity debiasing for collaborative recommendation. *Information Processing & Management* 58(1):102387.

Castells P, Hurley N, Vargas S (2021) Novelty and diversity in recommender systems. *Recommender Systems Handbook* (Springer), 603-646.

Chen J, Dong H, Wang X, Feng F, Wang M, He X (2023) Bias and debias in recommender system: A survey and future directions. *ACM Transactions on Information Systems* 41(3):1-39.

Cheng HK, Fan W, Guo P, Huang H, Qiu L (2020) Can "gold medal" online sellers earn gold? The impact of reputation badges on sales. *Journal of Management Information Systems* 37(4):1099-1127.

Farronato C, Fradkin A, MacKay A (2023) Self-preferencing at Amazon: evidence from search rankings. *AEA Papers and Proceedings* (American Economic Association 2014 Broadway, Suite 305, Nashville, TN 37203), 239-243.

Guo X, Wang L, Zhang M, Chen G (2023) First things first? Order effects in online product recommender systems. *ACM Transactions on Computer-Human Interaction* 30(1):1-35.

Häubl G, Trifts V (2000) Consumer decision making in online shopping environments: The effects of interactive decision aids. *Marketing Science* 19(1):4-21.

Häubl G, Dellaert BGC, Donkers B (2010) Tunnel Vision: Local Behavioral Influences on Consumer Decisions in Product Search. *Marketing Science* 29(3):438-455.

Jannach D, Lerche L, Zanker M (2018) Recommending based on implicit feedback. *Social Information Access* (Springer), 510-569.

Knijnenburg BP, Willemsen MC, Gantner Z, Soncu H, Newell C (2012) Explaining the user experience of recommender systems. *User modeling and user-adapted interaction* 22:441-504.

Lee D, Hosanagar K (2019) How do recommender systems affect sales diversity? A cross-category investigation via randomized field experiment. *Information Systems Research* 30(1):239-259.

--- (2021) How do product attributes and reviews moderate the impact of recommender systems through purchase stages? *Management Science* 67(1):524-546.

Li X, Grahl J, Hinz O (2022) How Do Recommender Systems Lead to Consumer Purchases? A Causal Mediation Analysis of a Field Experiment. *Information Systems Research* 33(2):620-637.

Melchiorre AB, Penz D, Ganhör C, Lesota O, Fragoso V, Fritzl F, Parada-Cabaleiro E, Schubert F, Schedl M (2023) Emotion-aware music tower blocks (EmoMTB): an intelligent audiovisual interface for music discovery and recommendation. *International Journal of Multimedia Information Retrieval* 12(1):13.

Peng J, Liang C (2023) On the Differences Between View-Based and Purchase-Based Recommender Systems. *MIS Quarterly* 47(2):875-900.

Sacharidis D (2020) Building user trust in recommendations via fairness and explanations. *Adjunct Publication of the 28th ACM Conference on User Modeling, Adaptation and Personalization*, 313-314.

Su X, Li P, Zhu X (2023) The Influence of Herd Mentality on Rating Bias and Popularity Bias: A Bi-Process Debiasing Recommendation Model Based on Matrix Factorization. *Behavioral Sciences* 13(1):63.

Wei F, Chen S, Jin J, Zhang S, Zhou H, Wu Y (2022) Adaptive alleviation for popularity bias in recommender systems with knowledge graph. *Security and Communication Networks* 2022(1):4264489.

Willemsen MC, Graus MP, Knijnenburg BP (2016) Understanding the role of latent feature diversification on choice difficulty and satisfaction. *User Modeling and User-Adapted Interaction* 26:347-389.

Xue L, Zhang P, Zeng A (2019) Enhancing the long-term performance of recommender system. *Physica A: Statistical Mechanics and its Applications* 531:121731.

Yalcin E, Bilge A (2022) Evaluating unfairness of popularity bias in recommender systems: A comprehensive user-centric analysis. *Information Processing & Management* 59(6):103100.

Yang Z, Zhang Z-K, Zhou T (2013) Anchoring bias in online voting. *Europhysics Letters* 100(6):68002.

Zhang M, Hurley N (2008) Avoiding Monotony: Improving the Diversity of Recommendation Lists. *Proceedings of the 2008 ACM Conference on Recommender Systems*, 123-130.

Zhao Z, Chen J, Zhou S, He X, Cao X, Zhang F, Wu W (2022) Popularity bias is not always evil: Disentangling benign and harmful bias for recommendation. *IEEE Transactions on Knowledge and Data Engineering*.